NO-ONE LIKES US, WE DON'T CARE

ANDREW WOODS

NO-ONE LIKES US, WE DON'T CARE

TRUE STORIES FROM MILLWALL, BRITAIN'S MOST NOTORIOUS FOOTBALL HOOLIGANS

JOHN BLAKE

Published by John Blake Publishing Ltd,
3 Bramber Court, 2 Bramber Road,
London W14 9PB, England

www.johnblakepublishing.co.uk

www.facebook.com/Johnblakepub facebook
twitter.com/johnblakepub twitter

First published in paperback in 2011

ISBN: 978-1-84358-330-1

British Library Cataloguing-in-Publication Data:

A catalogue record for this book is available from the British Library.

Design by www.envydesign.co.uk

Printed in Great Britain by CPI Group (UK) Ltd

7 9 10 8 6

Papers used by John Blake Publishing are natural, recyclable products
made from wood grown in sustainable forests. The manufacturing processes
conform to the environmental regulations of the country of origin.

Every attempt has been made to contact the relevant copyright-holders,
but some were unobtainable. We would be grateful if the appropriate people
could contact us.

AUTHORS' NOTE

A few of the chaps were sat around a table after a funeral. Another one of Millwall's original F-Troop had passed away, and with him had gone over forty years of tales. My 25 years paled into insignificance alongside some of the older chaps, with their stories from the early sixties.

Talk of a book had been quashed before. No one was interested in becoming famous, a celebrity hooligan, but we realised that time waits for no man and it was important that our stories were logged before being lost in history. So a few of us resolved to do something about it this time.

We needed a ghostwriter and were introduced to Andrew Woods. Over the following 12 months we met up with Andrew on many occasions. *No One Likes Us, We Don't Care* is the result of all of our meetings.

We would like to thank Andrew for all his effort and we look forward to working with him again on a follow-up book. We would especially like to thank Allie and all at John Blake, for their instant support and backing. Thanks are also due to all the fellas involved who added a lot of minor details, many of which hadn't been stored by some of our ageing memory banks, to

Suzi and June, without whom we would still be at the first draft stage, and to El Capitan Szotowicz, the old war veteran who entertained us with his war stories and provided a great place for us to work.

All of us Millwall fans felt that true stories about Millwall were long overdue, important and relevant. Our names are totally irrelevant. None of us involved in this book wants fame or glory or for any of us to take centre stage. Hence it is Andrew, our ghostwriter, whose name appears on the cover. Faceless hooligans we would all like to remain.

CONTENTS

*'Serious sport has nothing to do with fair play.
It is bound up with hatred, jealousy, boastfulness,
disregard of all rules and sadistic pleasure in witnessing
violence. In other words, it is war minus the shooting.'*

George Orwell

1

WE HEARD THE CHANT

We heard the chant:
'Leeds ... Leeds ... Leeds ... '

Somebody opened the doors of The Duke of Albany and ten of the Leeds Service Crew were walking past the pub. We shot out the doors and attacked. Eight of us steamed straight into them. My eyes locked on the one nearest to me. I ran at him and threw a right as hard as possible. It caught this geezer flush on the temple and he stumbled into one of his boys. So much had gone into that right that I stumbled over, too. I knew he'd been caught with a good 'un and, as I looked up, another five Millwall boys were running across the road towards us. The fella who I hit was heavily dazed. Two more of our firm came from behind me, and one of them punched him on the top of his head. The other kicked him in the leg, trying to take him down.

The Service Crew were surrounded. Punches and kicks were raining in. The Leeds boys were covering up, with just the odd one trying to throw a punch back. They were all backed up to each other in a tight little ball. Still no one was on the floor. Fifteen people throwing punches and kicking fuck out of them. It carried on for about ten seconds. Then one Leeds fan spotted a gap and they all made a dash for their lives, back towards the Old Kent Road. They were running through the hordes and taking kicks and punches until the pack swallowed them up and they disappeared out of my sight.

And now? Now I am involved. I am pumped up. Elated. The adrenalin is rushing through my body. My heart is pumping so fast it could keep ten men going. I have just thrown my first punch at an opposing fan. I am buzzing. It had all happened so quickly. Twenty seconds from hearing the chant to watching them sprint up the road. Twenty seconds that guaranteed the path I was going to take for more than the next twenty years. Yet it had seemed like it had all happened in slow motion. Concentrate! Hit! Don't get hit! Hit and don't get hit. We strolled back into the pub. And it is official. I am a hooligan.

It was a day that would never be forgotten. By me, at any rate. It was Saturday, 8 November 1986. Me, my two uncles and five of their firm were drinking in The Albany, a pub on the Monson Road about 200 yards from The Den. This was my official introduction to fighting at football. From fighting in the playgrounds to fighting in the pubs, this was a natural progression. From that day I was hooked. Being involved with the most feared, vicious, brutal and violent hooligan firm in the country is a buzz that cannot be given to you by any amount of drink or drugs. Any hooligan in the country deep down – deep down – wishes that he was born a Millwall fan. Anyone who denies it is a liar!

I had been going with my dad all season. In fact, I had been going with my dad for years. Every home game we would meet all his and my uncle's friends in the pub. My father totally abhorred all the violence at football. Yet the firm members were also members of his family and a lot of his friends. He was never involved in any of the fighting. For years, when the boys in the pub were leaving for some trouble, my dad would stay behind – making sure I stayed with him. No words were spoken. No lectures. No, 'Now listen, son, I don't want you to get involved with the firm, it's trouble, one day someone won't come back from one of these games!' Nothing like that. Nothing. Just a look. Maybe he could see the growing sense of intrigue and fascination within me. How my ears pricked up and my eyes lit up when the chaps in the firm were talking about some recent fight or other. Without saying it, it was very clear to me that my dad did not want me to join 'The Firm'.

He did not go that particular day. Me and my two uncles were there. My dad was working in a warehouse near the Old Kent Road. He was a storeman for a big stationery company and I knew he was going to start missing more and more games. Saturday was now overtime for him. Time-and-a-half. Sunday was double time. Times were tough. We weren't rolling about in money.

I had been building up to this day for a couple of years; on the fringe without being involved. On this day, my time had come. Simple as that. No one had put any pressure on me. No one told me to get involved. For years I had been in the firm's pub, drinking with them, hearing some stories. There was no recruitment process. It was now time to choose whether to just pile in with them, stay on the periphery, or back out totally. My time had come. Leeds were in town and everyone knew what that meant. A big club with a big following meant a big chance of a big ruck. We were drinking in the pub and had had a couple of pints when we first heard the chant.

Glasses hit the table and the race was on to get out. After the fight, everyone talked about it in the pub. We were laughing and joking, but only in our own little circles. No one was shouting

3

at the top of their voices. That's the Millwall way. You never know who could be standing next to you. This was clear to me long before I threw that first right-hand punch. No one said anything to me about my involvement. Everyone just went back to their drinks. Within a few minutes, the conversation had moved on and it was almost like it had never happened.

A couple of people came in and told us that Leeds were everywhere. Straight away, the atmosphere changed. Everyone readied themselves for the next bit of action. We started making our way to the ground. I didn't see any trouble outside the ground and I entered the Ilderton Road Stand, or 'The Halfway Line' as it was known. Not another thought about the fight entered my head. Now it was time to concentrate on the match – although it's a bit hard when you're that pissed. Fighting broke out across the pitch from me in the Cold Blow Lane end but nothing major.

After the match, we headed straight back to The Albany and back on the piss. I had a couple of pints there and walked on down the Old Kent Road to The Dun Cow. We stayed there drinking until my head was swimming so much I had to go home. I had just turned 13.

The club nearly went bust following my first involvement: 'MILLWALL FORCED TO MAKE HOME GAMES ALL-TICKET FOLLOWING FIGHTING WITH LEEDS'.

I didn't think too much about the press reports, nor about the repercussions – I was too busy buzzing off my first involvement as a hooligan. But we were forced by the Football League to make all home games all-ticket. How was that going to deter hooligans? We had met a few of The Service Crew as they came past our pub shouting, 'Leeds ... Leeds ... Leeds.'

What the fuck did it matter whether I had a ticket in my

pocket or not? Millwall lost a lot of revenue. Picture the scene – it's half-past two on a Saturday afternoon. Two geezers finish a job early.

'Fancy going football?'

'Can't … the ticket office will be shut by the time we get there.'

'Oh shite … forgot about that … let's go for a pint in a pub near the ground and see if we can kick the fuck out of some away fans instead then, eh?'

'Yeah, why not?'

See what I mean? All-ticket!

The average attendance went from 6,000 down to 3,200 after this piece of legislation. The average number of hooligans? Well, that just stayed the same. Everyone was still drinking in the pubs and milling around the ground on matchdays, even if they didn't go in. It was no great problem. Our tickets were always organised. One of us would go to the ticket office on Cold Blow Lane. Having to sort out a ticket is no real deterrent, is it? If anything, it just shows how slow the authorities were in dealing with the problem. For me and the chaps in our firm, it meant nothing.

Shortly after the legislation kicked in, we played Portsmouth at The Den. Pompey fans were everywhere. Five of us had a right tear-up with five of them. I had a one-on-one with this fella – tall, skinny geezer. I kicked him in the leg, and he didn't really move. So I punched him straight in the mouth. That stunned him. I grabbed him by his collar, and he caught me a couple on the head. I threw about seven punches – all smack on the button. One right on his eye. His nose didn't bust but that boy went back to Portsmouth sporting one hell of a big black eye. The Old Bill jumped in and we all faded into the crowd. The ticket in my pocket? The ticket was fine. Not even crumpled.

2

FROM THE ELEPHANT
TO THE DEN

I was born in October 1946 at the Elephant & Castle in south-east London. Ours was a big, traditional, working-class family and I had five brothers and two sisters. We all lived on one floor of an old Victorian house. Life for everyone was hard. There was no money about. My clothes were always hand-me-downs or what my mother made. That was also how she made a bit of extra money, doing alterations and a bit of sewing for other people. My old man was never about. He was either working on the boats on the River Thames as a lighterman or in the pub pissed.

My first introduction into following Millwall was from my older brother. He and his mates used to go regularly. I started tagging along at 14 years of age. My first game was in 1960 against York City at home. I will never forget that Saturday. It was freezing cold, a week before Christmas. Me, my brother and two of his mates left our house at the Elephant and walked to the ground. The Den. The thing that always stuck in my mind was the size of the crowd inside the ground. It probably wasn't that big a crowd on the day, maybe 6,000–7,000, but to a 14-year-old boy it was massive.

6

We were behind the goal in the Cold Blow Lane end. I couldn't believe the surging and swaying, never mind the crowd's reaction when we scored. Big crowds were not new to me; I was used to being in and around the local markets trying to nick whatever I could get my hands on to feed myself or make some money from, but this was different. This was a different world to me. From that day, I was hooked. My priority through the week was to feed myself and have enough money for the football – which I got through selling scrap metal or thieving.

There was always trouble at the football – before, during and after the game with the opposing fans. In the Sixties, you wouldn't get big numbers of away fans coming to The Den and, with no segregation, you could easily go to an away game and not get spotted if you had your wits about you. When a group of away fans were spotted, they would get a hiding. Our favourite trick was to ask someone who we suspected was an away fan for directions to a local pub or station. A funny accent or the wrong answer? Bang! They would cop an unfortunate one (a punch in the head). Long after the match, local disputes would be settled in the pubs. So violence was always a part of life for me, from getting the cane at school to getting a backhander off the old man when he was pissed, or fighting people on the streets. Violence at football was just an extension of normal life. Violence was the norm.

My first away game was at Crystal Palace. We made the short journey to Selhurst Park in South Norwood. It was a Friday night match – a good night out, fun on the train, laughing and joking. No trouble. We won 2–0.

The first time I remember a team actually bringing down a mob looking for trouble was Brighton in September 1964. There were about 20 of us hanging about outside New Cross Station. This mob of blokes came out of the station and we just thought they were Millwall. There were about 40 of them. This big cunt with a big mop of blond hair said to my mate, 'You Millwall?'

My mate replied without thinking, 'Yeah.'

Crack! He nutted my mate straight on the nose. Now, at the time, I used to carry one of those wooden Old Bill truncheons about with me, probably about 10in long, which I used to keep in the lining of my overcoat. I pulled it out and hit the geezer straight over the swede. I felt his head split. He groaned and went down on one knee. My mate that was reeling from the headbutt came back and kneed him straight in his face. He fell back on to the floor in a ball. We went to town on him, me with my bat and my mate stamping. There was fighting going on all around me. After the beating, the fella on the floor stopped moving. He was out cold, claret pissing out the top of his head! The blood turned his blond hair into a brown mess.

We were now looking for our next victim. Beside us two of my brother's mates were fighting with two fellas. We steamed into them and I hit one across the back with my trusted truncheon. He stumbled forward. Then there was a blood-curdling scream! Everyone stopped for a second. One of my mates, who was a right nutter, had pulled out a cut-throat razor and striped one of them down his face. The sight of this geezer holding his face and screaming caused panic. Everyone just started running off towards the Old Kent Road.

You get asked, 'Who do you support?' When you say Millwall, people's faces change. Usually shock. It's a good feeling not to be a normal glory-hunter following United or Arsenal. Millwall hooligans are real football fans. We're even more passionate than other fans because we will fight for our club and territory.

When we had the firm in the Seventies, we would go to away

games and everyone would know each other. All of F-Troop would be regularly drinking down the Old Kent Road and living in the surrounding areas of Peckham, Walworth, Bermondsey and Deptford. It was a relatively small community but I think those numbers worked in our favour as everyone knew each other. If you came up against another firm, you couldn't run because you knew everyone you were with. So if you turned and ran, you could never show your face again on your manor. We could take on firms four times our size because no one would take a backward step. This must have done other firms' heads in. We had some amazing results on the terraces when we numbered 100, sometimes 200 at a push. We took the home ends of Oxford, Pompey, Bristol Rovers, Bristol City, Blackpool, Sheffield Wednesday, Norwich and Chelsea. With small numbers, we were ferocious. The banter was blinding and there were some proper comedians.

The thing was that most people would be up to no good during their normal lives. I don't mean they were all bank robbers; they were just bending the rules and not like some of these cunts today, mugging people or breaking into houses. These lads were just duckers and divers – sort of Del Boy types. You have got to realise that in the Sixties and Seventies there was no segregation, something that would put the fear of God into today's arm-waving hooligan.

With players, all we want is 100 per cent. The player for me who typified the Millwall spirit was Frank Neary; he was shit but he would give 100 per cent every time he pulled that shirt on. He was a big old lump who played up front. If he didn't have the ball, he wouldn't stop running until he got it back. I mean you don't get that with the modern-day footballer, they're just overpaid poofs. We have always had players at Millwall that have had the Millwall spirit – Cripps, Kitchener, Hurlock,

Steven – but I think this will become a thing of the past with the emergence of the modern-day mercenary footballer. For me, the new ground made it easy for opponents – it's not intimidating and it's too big for us. I mean, for big games you still get an intimidating atmosphere but, for a midweek game against a small club, we have lost the advantage.

3

THE HAMMERS GET HAMMERED

It was 4 May 1972.

I smacked him over the head with a hammer. He fell to the floor and three of us kicked him in the head and body a fair few times. He was gurgling. Yes, West Ham had crossed the river.

The rivalry goes back to Millwall's origins on the Isle of Dogs in East London. It continued when we moved across the river to New Cross, south-east London. It's like the Krays versus the Richardsons, with West Ham's ICF firm being the Krays, the east London, media-hungry, star-struck celebrity-seekers. We were Millwall's faceless hooligans, the Richardsons, the south-east London equivalent. Getting on with the job and trying to avoid the glare of the media and notoriety. Cass Pennant, the famous ICF and Millwall's faceless hooligans. Anyone in the know can tell who the real deal is in these comparisons.

We called them the Ice Cream Firm because they just melted away. I suppose you could call the Seventies and Eighties West Ham's heyday. We had some good rucks with them in those days. In 1972, we were outside The Den waiting for them. We clashed in the street and they came off second best. The famous

ICF ran into the empty home end seeking refuge before the start of the game. We had them trapped. They used pick-axe handles, hammers and wrenches to gain a brief advantage – or really just to keep us from crawling all over them. The game kicked off but most of us didn't even notice. We had the ICF stuck at the back of the stand and we were on the attack. They defended themselves for 90 minutes – and for the ICF, it was 90 minutes of hell. At the final whistle, they managed to make it out on to the street outside the ground. The Old Bill sent in the horses but they still had to get to the station and they ran the gauntlet of continuous attacks. They were finally saved when they got to the station.

Three hours of constant fighting. All this at a testimonial for Harry Cripps. We all went for a pint down the Old Kent Road.

A couple of years later, we had an away match at Upton Park. We took a good firm that day, all ready for a tear-up. When we arrived, there was a big reception party for us and fighting broke out everywhere. West Ham were run ragged on their own turf by 1,000 Millwall. We were the top firm.

And that was still true in 1978/79, when we knew West Ham would be coming into Bank station. We were about 100-strong as the train pulled in. As soon as the doors opened, we attacked, trapping them on the train. They were trying to escape, shouting and screaming. One West Ham got stabbed. We found out later he didn't make it. We were held at King's Cross station by the Old Bill; we had a few stragglers outside and heard the fighting. Around 400 West Ham were outside the station. We managed to get through the Old Bill and we had about 400 ourselves by now so it was even numbers.

As we got there, we all split up. The Millwall that were ambushed outside were taking a hiding. Two others helped me pull two West Ham off one Millwall and got them up against a bus. One was hit with a lump of wood. He hit the floor instantly. The other one followed him to the floor. A knee in the head saw to that. Later, someone said they had seen these two being helped into a black cab. A trip to the hospital, no doubt.

The Old Bill were nowhere to be seen. I suppose they thought they would let us get on with it. We then saw five West Ham dart down a side road, so we sprinted after them. They ran into a pub arming themselves with glasses and ashtrays, throwing them to hold us back. We steamed them with stools and tables. They were trapped against the bar and taking a beating before they scrambled over and – with barmaids screaming – they shot out the back.

Making our way back to the station, we picked off a few more West Ham on the way. A good result that day.

A few years later, in 1984, we clashed again. West Ham were playing Palace that day and we knew they would be coming. They were spotted at New Cross Station with a massive firm. We got ready. They came running up the road and were sent running back down it just as quick – back into the station behind the safety of the Old Bill.

West Ham were set on revenge after this humiliation and, shortly after, they attacked us with a petrol bomb at London Bridge. They needed to try to even things up because toe-to-toe they were not quite up to it.

Come the Nineties, their firm was non-existent. Since then, they have never got together a firm to take on Millwall. One of the funniest incidents occurred at The Den, when Millwall won 4–1. We were trapped in the corner by the Old Bill and we were goading West Ham to come on to the pitch. This was followed by a quality comedy moment as none of them wanted to be the first on the pitch; they were all holding each other back. Brave boys.

It is probably because nowadays they are more likely to be a poncey Essex boy rather than an East End boy. Also, if you ask a modern-day West Ham fan who their biggest rivals are, they would say Spurs. They obviously don't know their history. One of their firm, Cass Pennant, has gone on to carve out a career telling his stories. They made a film about his life which wasn't bad, albeit a bit far-fetched at the end. Especially as he tried to tie his shooting in with his football past. He worked on the door of the Albany Empire Club in Deptford, south-east London, a club used by many young Millwall, where there was trouble most weekends. Cass and his bouncers rarely went inside the club, usually only to clear up the aftermath of a fight. In the film, he made out it was some trouble with Arsenal, when, in truth, he had picked on a hot-headed clubber. Nothing to do with football firms.

After what seemed like years of inactivity by the ICF, we started hearing little snippets of them making a comeback. Nothing against us, of course. The first attempt by them that hit the headlines was in October 2003. They were away at Tottenham – it was a mid-week Carling Cup clash against their London 'rivals', so they didn't have too far to travel on that occasion – and apparently they attacked The Cockerel Pub on Tottenham High Road. Ninety-three West Ham were arrested for causing extensive damage. Some were also arrested at nearby Northumberland Park train station for criminal damage and violent disorder.

A couple of years later, they travelled to Italy. The night before a UEFA Cup clash against Palermo in September 2006, an hour-long battle occurred between the two sets of fans. It appears, reading between the lines and having heard a few whispers, that they were very small in number. All the same, 20 West Ham fans were arrested following the incident in which 17 people – six West Ham and five police officers – suffered injuries. So six of them and six Palermo took a pasting.

In July 2008, the ICF travelled to America and trouble occurred during a pre-season friendly with MLS side Columbus Crew. West Ham fans entered a corner of the stadium in which the home side's supporters were gathered and fighting broke out, requiring police and stadium security staff to intervene. So maybe the ICF were indeed making a comeback. We had hoped so for years … and hoped we could draw them in a Cup game.

And eventually, we did. Four years and thirty-six days since our last game, along came a Tuesday night Cup tie against Essex's finest. Everyone would be coming out the woodwork for this one. The meet for us was kept a secret up until the last minute. The day before the game, word went round that we would meet at Blackhorse Road. A few of us met at All Bar One in Leicester Square in the afternoon; we had a few beers then made our way to Blackhorse Road on the Tube. West Ham had been told where the meet would be, out the way of the Old Bill. By the time everyone had arrived, we had about 250, a proper firm, most of Wall's finest hooligans from down the years. This was to be a battle to decide who was the best out of the two firms. West Ham's chance to save some face.

But they didn't show up. We waited right until the last minute, until we had to leave or we'd miss the game. We had been waiting probably three or four hours. All that time, since the first 'Wall had arrived at the pre-arranged meeting point, only for them not to show.

A few days later, West Ham claimed that, by the time they had got there, we had gone. Now we were only a few miles from Upton Park – I know London traffic is bad and the trains are unreliable, but four hours to travel a few miles? Come on.

We now took the initiative. We were going to find them. We

made our way overland, got out at Wood Grange station and headed for The Queen's, which is their main pub. Someone had got in touch with them and told them we were on our way after we left Blackhorse Road. We gave them the route we would be taking so they could meet us on the way. Nothing. No reception. We were marching about at West Ham while they either hid in pubs or threw bottles at the Old Bill. Now, we could have gone on the rampage but we were determined to get to The Queen's pub without Old Bill attention. That was the easy way; bash a few West Ham fans, get wrapped up by the Old Bill and claim we had done the West Ham mob. That was the old ICF way. Not ours. We wanted their proper firm.

After phone calls to say where we were, the Old Bill got on to us. Full riot police. Surrounded. We were now wrapped up. Makes you wonder how the Old Bill knew our position. Did the West Ham boys tip them off because they knew they couldn't match us?

As we got closer to the ground, we were led across some sort of park or open space, and then some Ham finally appeared. After hours of waiting about, they popped up behind the safety of the Old Bill, with the usual arm-waving and the odd missile coming our way. As we got to the ground, we bumped into a few of the youth who had had an off with some West Ham and given them a hiding. I think that night West Ham were happy to pick off any straggler and claim a victory. I spoke to another older lad who took a tidy little firm and they dealt with anything put in front of them.

In the ground, there was the usual aggro with the Old Bill and stewards. When we scored, we went mental. If you could bottle that feeling you would be a millionaire. Right up until they equalised, I thought we would nick it. Then a load of fat men in replica shirts invaded the pitch. In the corner, there were about

200 West Ham and eight stewards. Comical. How can they hold you back?

We were hemmed in the away end three deep by riot Old Bill. Couldn't go anywhere. The West Ham that came on to the pitch didn't come near us. After the game, we were escorted out of east London. The West Ham fans rioted into the night in their replica shirts. The next few days, the ICF propaganda machine claimed that, when they got to Blackhorse Road, we had gone. They also claimed victory in fights around the ground, with one outrageous claim that a mob from Gravesend, north Kent, had been running around south-east London bashing up Millwall fans. Well done to you all.

The truth? There was a pre-arranged meet; West Ham never showed. With 'Wall's main firm, they were happy to stand behind the Old Bill, throw bottles and stab innocent fans in replica shirts. Says it all.

4

HOOKED

I was born into a large Millwall-supporting family – uncles, cousins, father – all of us living around the Old Kent Road, Bermondsey and Peckham. They are areas that the south London press reported had been red-flagged by the US State Government as places that should be avoided at all costs, as dangerous as Guatemala, Latin America, where death squads are commonplace.

Going with them all to the match are some of my first memories. Going to the game as a six-year-old kid with the full boozers, the smell of the pubs, beer and fags was soon a religion. Every home game we'd be in The Duke of Albany before and after the match. I had started drinking in The Albany at 11. Shandies to begin with, then I'd be slipped the odd pint of lager here and there. By my thirteenth birthday, I was a fully-fledged member of the drinking fraternity.

In our drinking round, every week there would be a whip. All of the fellas would throw in … well, as a school kid, I didn't know how much they would all throw in each. I was just grateful for all the free drinks. My uncles and father were obviously well respected because none of the boys ever questioned my free drinks from their hard-earned money. This must have gone on for over a year, until my uncles and dad started giving me a few pounds each at the door before we went in. Now when we entered, my £5 whip was paid like all the men. I was 13 years of age, 5ft 10in and weighing 13st. Boxing in the gym a couple of times a week and playing football. Drinking in the pub with the boys for a couple of years. A big, fit boy for my age.

School at this time had very much taken a back seat. That didn't happen overnight; it was more of a natural progression. At this stage, I had been doing the occasional day here and there labouring. Five quid for a day and then king for a night – straight to the pub after work. Fuck maths, chemistry and biology – give me Fosters, Tennants and Hoffmeisters! Soon, school was just a memory and full time on building sites was how my days were spent. I'll never forget my first full week on £5 a day, £25 for the week.

No more subsidies were necessary; my whip had been coming out of my own pocket for a year now. Still a fiver a whip. Twenty men in our firm, £100 every home game in The Albany. That was just our firm. There were around 150 men crammed into that pub for each match. The old manager must have been doing more than OK. He was obviously a tough old cookie. There was trouble at every home game, often just outside the pub, but the landlord had a lot of respect. The chaps looked after their pub, too – this was our second home. No one was going to allow anything to happen to The Albany.

For a start, there was our firm drinking in there, and anywhere from three to four other firms drinking in there, too. Not to mention many other individuals, not connected to any of the firms. These were people clearly not intimidated by the presence of 100 of Millwall's hardcore hooligans. Locals – The

Albany was their home, too. Yes, no one was going to let anyone take liberties in The Albany. Nothing, to my recollection, ever happened to our second home.

So at 14 years of age, my drinking in the pub had been going on for three years. Before and after every home game, often then down the Old Kent Road, I was mixing and mingling with the top boys of all the firms. And I felt comfortable. My first match was against Oldham on Saturday, 4 November 1978. I can remember it being freezing cold but, once inside, all the heat of the bodies soon warmed me up. I could not really see a lot but, when we scored, the noise was deafening. That roar of the crowd. I was desperate for us to score again to hear that noise. We did. Wow! I was hooked. Football was going to be a big part of my life.

I suppose my dad just thought I was old enough to go to the game, or my mum told him to take me to get me out from under her feet. The overriding memory is of my dad coming out with the right hump. Oldham beat us 3–2. The scowling faces, the passion of my father, the atmosphere, the noise and shouting, the swaying of the crowd, the amount of people in that one place, the roar when the teams come out and when a goal went in and being in the pub all totally hooked me from day one. Sensible men went completely out of control, while mild-mannered men underwent complete personality changes, like my father. The highs and the lows. I remember those early days, treading on eggshells around my dad after a loss because he was pissed off. Leeds on 8 November 1986 was the major turning point. By 14, it had become total involvement. At 17, I was a fully-fledged member of the most notorious, violent, vicious and downright evil football firm in the country – The Bushwackers. And I loved it. Aggro was always a part of any game, whether it was opposing fans, players or officials on the receiving end. The Den was always all about intimidation.

A major thing for me had been the events at Kenilworth Road in March 1985. Everyone coming back from the game, buzzing. It had been a big game for us, the quarter-finals of the Cup. That was the reason the numbers were there. Ten thousand following our then third-division team against a first-division team in Luton Town. How disgraceful it was, the scandal of Millwall's hooligans. I can remember all the headlines and soundbites.

Obviously, it was a major national issue. For weeks, everywhere you went it was all anyone seemed to be talking about. How great it had been down there. What each person had been doing and getting up to on the day. The Luton fans having a go in the ground; the police charges; the rioting in the town centre. Everyone in school was talking about it, too. People in school whose elder brothers had gone and had come back were regaling the younger ones with tales of their firm. One kid's brother had headbutted a Luton fan and he went through a glass window. I thought that was quality.

Everyone was talking about it. I remember thinking, 'Why can't I go?' Well, it was a night game and I was only 11. My dad wouldn't let me go. I had been travelling on away days for a few years, but only on Saturdays. I'd never been allowed to go to a night game. That first away game was 7 November 1981. I had been on at my dad to take me away for ages. He finally relented and said he would take me to Swindon. Fucked if I knew where Swindon was. All I knew was where we lived and our little area. I couldn't wait.

We went to the Elephant & Castle station; Tube to Paddington. Full of Millwall on the train; bottles of beer and light ale scattered all over it; the cabin full of cigarette smoke and songs all the way to Swindon. This was totally different from a home game. Fields ... cows ... trains ... fields ... fields and fields.

My dad, my uncle and a couple of their mates were playing cards on the train. One of my dad's mates got cleaned out – he was devastated. It all got a bit heated. No fighting, though. Kaluki they were playing. It's like a seven-card brag game. It's so fucking complicated – I still don't understand the game today!

We eventually arrived and walked to the ground. It seemed like ages. My dad carried me on his shoulders half the way. I remember looking round and seeing lots of Millwall walking up. We got into the ground and on to the terrace and I was stood next to my dad. The pitch seemed massive. They had picked their spot and I went for a wander down to the front of the terrace. There were no cages – I could have jumped over and run on to the pitch. We had taken a couple of hundred, I would think. Not that many that I couldn't have found my dad again. You don't really notice the facilities at that age; you probably think every stadium is fantastic but, having been back since that day, I know now that it's a shit-hole, too.

We won 2–1 and with all that excitement, all those hours travelling and all that walking, I fell asleep on the train back to Paddington. The whole experience was great. I would have loved to have gone to every away game, but I suppose finances restricted my dad's away trips. Not that we were thinking about those things as eight-year-old kids. But just like after my first home game, I was hooked.

'The night football changed', they called it. Luton even banned all away fans from that point for four years. 'Outrage' ... 'Disgrace to football'. The boys in the pub didn't seem to think so. Neither did I. I was glued to the never-ending TV footage. Recognising some of the faces from the pub on *Match of the Day* was a big buzz, too. Watching the television and actually recognising some of the faces from our pub. Listening to them all talk. Standing there, still on my shandies with the occasional pint cheekily chucked in. Thinking – fuck, I wish I had been there!

Journalist Jim Murray reported to his London newspaper, 'As a lifelong Millwall supporter, I could only stand in disbelief as I watched the riots and I felt like crying ... as a true Millwall fan, it was impossible not to feel shame, not to feel sorrow for the game of football and not to despair at how low life had sunk. For these were not fans, they were not people, they were animals.'

That was pretty much what my dad said as he watched the pictures being replayed day after day. No way was I telling him what was in my mind: 'Wow ... what fuckin' great fun! '

A lot of people were concerned about the cramming in at the away end, not using it as an excuse, but saying that they hadn't seen anything like that for years. My father was appalled, saying around the dinner table that it was a disgrace, an embarrassment to the club, the worst thing they had ever done. He was not alone; the majority of Millwall fans agreed with him. The vast majority of Millwall fans do not agree with the hooliganism. Me? On and after 13 March 1985, I was fucking excited ... and gutted not to have been there. The stories that everyone was coming back with ... well, I was an impressionable kid growing up on the tough streets of south-east London. That night made a big, big impression on me. The Night Football Changed – it was for me. It was the night I, and many other kids of my age group, decided we wanted to be involved in this.

5

SWINGING
THE BLUES

We've had a few good laughs at the expense of Chelsea over the years. The stand-out ones, though, have to be when we took over their pub and, not content with that, we took over The Shed. Fucking funny. It was in the Seventies and we weren't the fashion followers or designer junkies all the boys of today are. It was all flares and dodgy, checked shirts with long collars – blending in was not going to be a problem.

It was 12 February 1977 and we had a meet at the Charlie Chaplin pub at the Elephant & Castle; we had arranged it so that we could go over early. It was decided that we would get a Tube to King's Road and set ourselves up in the Chelsea Drugs Store, a pub on the corner of Royal Avenue and the King's Road. Once inside, the barman said, 'You boys are early,' obviously thinking we were Chelsea. There were only about 30 of us, F-Troop's finest at that time – Harry the Dog and all the boys.

We headed for the top floor and there was a DJ playing punk rock music. A good few beers had been supped and everyone was buzzing, the clock was ticking and we were ready. We had been in there a while when Chelsea's top boys came in. It is

24

possible that the name The Bushwackers was born out of this little tactic of ours, of laying in wait to ambush the other firm.

They soon came up the stairs to see what was going on. One of the lads said there was a private party but they could come in if they paid a fee, which they did. Once up the stairs, we attacked and kicked fuck out of them and threw them back down the stairs with everyone laughing. After a few more drinks, we left for the ground. They hadn't come back and we headed down the King's Road. We approached a wedding where the bride and groom were punks and, as we passed, a big shout of 'Millwall' went up. All the punks started shouting abuse and spitting at us. We steamed into them and left them in a heap. Their wedding photos must have looked good.

It was couple of years later when we decided to take over The Shed. A few of us had met up and talked about the best way to do it; it was like a fucking military operation organising it – getting everyone to meet up, travelling across London and all going to the home end. It was pay on the turnstiles then and everyone knew the plan. There were only a couple of hundred of us anyway but we had all split up as we walked around the ground. We didn't want anything to go wrong with our masterplan. Finally, we made our way to the Chelsea home end – our tactic of splitting into small groups so as not to draw too much attention to ourselves had worked a treat so far. We also figured that, when the fighting started, it would give us an advantage as we could come from different directions.

We stood there in silence. It seemed like an age. Then an almighty roar went up – it was off. Fighting broke out everywhere. It caught Chelsea completely by surprise. Most ran to the back of the stand for safety but some were standing and fighting. The ones left were obviously their game boys but, with us getting on top, the Old Bill came steaming in with batons and split us up. As the Chelsea firm joined the rest of them at the back of the stand, we were pushed down the terrace on to the running track that went around Stamford Bridge at the time. After the game, we made our way to The Britannia but there was no more action; the Chelsea boys had clearly had enough. And we even got a point that day in a 1–1 draw.

We had another early meet in The Charlie Chaplin because Chelsea were coming down for the first leg of a Milk Cup tie on 26 September 1984, and then we'd meet again on 9 October. The fighting started in the Elephant & Castle before the game. It continued after the match on Waterloo Bridge and one police officer was bottled.

In the return leg, Chelsea's Bobby Issac was stabbed outside the ground by Millwall fans and, after the game, we tried to smash down a police cordon to get at them. The police charged us and we turned on them, raining missiles at them on the Old Kent Road. We attacked as they took Chelsea away from the ground and the Old Bill sustained a few casualties. Chelsea were blocking the Old Kent Road so the ambulances couldn't take their injured away. Police reinforcements finally started to push us back but the fighting continued for half-an-hour all up New Cross Gate and the Old Kent Road.

We have had some fun with Chelsea, like the time we took 5,000 to Stamford Bridge in February 1985 for an FA Cup tie. Once inside the ground, we attacked the East Stand. Chelsea did not put up a fight, just turned and ran. We won the match 3–2 and knew Chelsea would be outside The Shed end waiting for revenge. So we waited inside the ground for the crowd to disperse – obviously, whoever was left behind would be Chelsea's top boys. Six hundred of us made our way round to The Shed and we were met by their firm. As before, they were given a good hiding and they had it on their toes. We followed them to The Gunter pub. Finally, Chelsea tried to stand their ground for a bit. In the end, it was the same result – they took a good hiding and a fair old kicking.

Then in January 1995, after beating Arsenal in the previous round of the FA Cup and running them ragged, we could not believe our luck – Chelsea in the next. We were sure there would be fireworks. The game itself was a bit of a let-down – a 0–0 draw. Worse than that, the Old Bill had the 18,573 in attendance completely under control with a heavy, heavy presence.

The replay was a lot more fun – Wednesday, 8 February. Before the game, we met at London Bridge. Our ticket allocation was sold out and we probably had around 4,000 that night. A quarter of those were looking for a right old tear-up. We jumped the Tube to the King's Road. Packed full of Millwall. The second we stepped back into the open air, we were surrounded by the Old Bill. Escorted straight into the ground, no opportunity for anything to occur. Unusual night for me, one of the few occasions that I was sober as a judge. I'd been working up the West End, straight home, changed and off to London Bridge. Not even time for a quick pint.

Once inside the ground, it was bouncing. Chelsea … FA Cup … night game … near full house … cracking atmosphere. The match went to extra time with the score 1–1. Still the teams could not be separated. Penalties … we won 5-4 and were jumping up and down celebrating like lunatics. Chelsea invaded the pitch at the other end of the ground. The result was forgotten instantly; something else kicked in. Chelsea were on the pitch; they wanted to have a go at us.

Around 80 of us ran on to the pitch from the away end. Over a little wall and ready for a proper tear-up. Must have been ten mounted police at the front within seconds and they were organising Old Bill shoulder to shoulder across the width of the pitch. They quickly managed to get in between us and stopped us from getting at each other en masse. A few slipped past them and some scuffles broke out, but the Old Bill soon had things under control. It's virtually impossible to get past them when it's like that.

We all turned round and headed back into the stand, mingling in straight away, and made our way outside the ground. Chelsea were waiting for us. We steamed into them, spreading them all over. Fights were breaking out everywhere. We were joined by the rest of Millwall from the away end. It's difficult in a situation like that to stick figures on how many of us and how many of them. No time to do the maths. But you do know that there are no innocents in situations like this. Anyone who's not interested would rapidly get the fuck out of there, so those who are left standing there are obviously looking for a tear-up.

I saw this one fella. He tried to stand his ground, but I steamed straight into him. He threw a couple of big right haymakers. I stepped back from both of them. Concentrate ... hit ... don't get hit ... hit ... don't get hit. As I ducked back from the second one, I stepped back in. Bang. A big right. Caught him flush on the side of the head. He did not like that. He turned tail and ran.

He was the catalyst. A few of them saw this and they ran, too, causing panic and even more to have it on their toes. Fighting was still going on around me and we easily had the upper hand. A couple of police on horseback steamed in and the Old Bill had soon restored order. It was now time to get the fuck out of there. Stick around to admire your handiwork and get arrested, or fall back into the crowd. The security and anonymity of the masses. It's easy to get lost in the crowd. We had the upper hand and really the police saved Chelsea from a worse beating. They surrounded us and we were escorted back to King's Road Tube station. Packed on to the train and away we go. On a night like that, they run the train through three or four stations without stopping. They want us the fuck away from the ground and out of Chelsea.

We got back to London Bridge and about 20 of us headed in to Garfunkel's, a bar on the station concourse at the entrance. My first pint of the day. It tasted sweet. No one had any injuries. A couple of commuters were in there, the odd office bod with half-an-hour to kill before his train. And us. We had a couple of pints and jumped the train back to South Bermondsey. No one had left and we all piled into The Bramcote Arms on the Bonamy estate. We had a few more in there. Nothing too late; work in the morning. All in all, a good night out at The Bridge.

6

GUNNING FOR TROUBLE

We had drawn Arsenal in the Cup. Everyone was buzzing with the idea of a trip to Highbury to see what Arsenal had to offer. After some careful planning, we decided to go straight into their manor and put on a good show. We knew that their boys would be drinking in The Arsenal Tavern, one of their main pubs. We set off on the Saturday morning with a tidy firm that was no more than 30-strong. Yet everyone was a proper chap and everyone knew each other. It was better that way because, when it kicked off, there was no confusion over who was who.

We got to north London and just round the corner from The Arsenal Tavern we gathered for a team talk. Our plan was to get in the pub by going in three or four at a time. When we were all in, it would kick off. Me and two of my mates went in and started playing pool. Looking about there were most of their top boys in here. Great, because they were about to meet 30 of ours. We mingled in with all the normal fans and little pockets of us were all over the pub. You are pretending to play pool but the adrenalin is flowing and we are waiting for the shout. It soon comes. Every little group of us had our targets in site.

'Miiilllwall ... '

Someone threw a pint glass behind the jump [bar] and we were away. The pool cues in our hands were now being used to attack a group of Arsenal standing by the pool table. I hit one across the nose and blood poured from it straight away. Someone hit him with a bottle and he collapsed in a heap. As I looked around, there were bodies everywhere and smashed glass all over the floor. There were people lying on the floor screaming while getting kicked and cut by the glass underneath them. It was like a Wild West pub fight – chairs being hit off people's heads but not smashing like the films, just people hitting the floor from the weight of the heavy stools.

Tables were turned over by some Arsenal trying to escape out of the front door. I pulled one of them back, grabbed on to his shirt and hit him around the side of the head with a pint glass I had just picked up. He fell to the floor in a ball, not moving. He was either spark out or thought he'd play dead until it was all over. The air was filled with people moaning and screaming. Any time anyone moved, I heard the sound of breaking glass. For a split second, we all stood still and surveyed the scene before rushing out of the pub.

As we came out, I tried to move my hand but couldn't feel my fingers. When I had glassed the fellow, the glass had sliced my hand open and my finger tips were dripping with blood. I kept walking away from the pub because I was no use to anyone with a busted hand, plus it would not take Poirot to work out I had just come from the pub with loads of Gooners cut to ribbons.

On the bus away from Arsenal, my hand was clenched tight in my pocket. By the time I got back home to Walworth, it looked like a big, fucked-up cricket ball. Fucking great fun, though. The whole plan from start to finish had worked a fucking treat. The Arsenal Tavern and all who drank in her had been smashed up good.

Monday, 10 January 1994 – we had drawn Arsenal in the FA Cup at The New Den. The season before, we had played them in the League Cup. With a sell-out crowd on a cold winter's night, we fancied our chances. We held our own but they scored right at the end after Kasey Keller was fouled. So we were looking to get some revenge on the Arsenal fans. A small group of us made our way up Ilderton Road towards the Old Kent Road. As we turned the corner, there was a group of Arsenal hooligans being herded by the police, certainly not enough to keep us from getting at each other.

There were about ten coppers, twenty Arsenal and fifteen of us. The ones at the front, about four or five of us, ran straight at the Arsenal. They braced themselves for an attack. All those at the front got a few lefts and rights in but, before any real damage could get done, the Old Bill on horses came in and broke it up. The police numbers were now enough to control the situation. The mounted police charged into us to disperse us and we jumped over a little metal fence into a small park and made our way out the gates and off round the back streets. We had just been involved in a fight. Old Bill found us and they nicked us; they escorted Arsenal to safety.

It was almost exactly a year later when, for the third year running, we drew Arsenal again in a Cup competition. We hoped to get a result third time lucky and, after being robbed the season before, we were fired up. Once again, we provided a hostile atmosphere for our north London rivals, with Ian Wright getting some serious stick. The Arsenal chant of 'Ian Wright-Wright-Wright' was hijacked by Millwall and turned into 'Ian Wank-Wank-Wank'. The abuse Wright and the other Arsenal players received throughout the game really levelled things up on the pitch. The match ended 0–0 with us having some good chances.

After the game, we went to The Jolly Gardeners on Rotherhithe New Road to try and cut off the escort. As they got near the pub, we went outside, ready to attack. However, the police had got the situation under control, keeping Arsenal back and us outside the pub. Then the sky lit up. Arsenal had fired a flare at us and it just whistled past the geezer's head next to me. It was still burning on the floor outside the pub.

The police contained us there while they escorted Arsenal to Surrey Quays station. We did not want to leave it there and decided to go after them. Our mob of about 40 went into Southwark Park and used the dark of the park to keep hidden from the main road. We headed to Surrey Quays to make our way to Whitechapel station, thinking Arsenal would be waiting for us. On arrival, we ran off the train and up the platform – we were rushing out of the station and came under a barrage of missiles, bottles, bricks and another flare. They had managed to arm themselves with anything they could get their hands on while waiting for us. We ran towards them, all the time coming under heavy bombardment. They were being held back by the police on Whitechapel Road. They kept us apart by hitting us back with truncheons and shields while the missiles from Arsenal were still coming. The Old Bill pushed us still further back towards Whitechapel Hospital. We were getting nicked now as they had started to handcuff a few of our boys while they had us pinned to the railings of the hospital.

Some Arsenal had broken through the police lines on the opposite side of the road. The coppers holding us panicked, opening up a gap, and we saw our chance. Three of us shot through. We jumped over the railings into the road, then jumped the second set of railings to face the mob. As we landed, their mob scattered. We chased a small group of about eight down Fulbourne Street. Three of them stopped to front us and one of them came at me. As he got close, I threw a big uppercut, connecting straight on the chin. He went down like a sack of shit.

From behind me, I heard, 'Stop! Police!' Head down, I started sprinting. I had just slipped away from them once and there was no way they were catching me. I was gone. No idea how long the police chased me for; you do not stop and look behind you in those situations. You run. You get away, then you worry about where you are later. You don't care about the fact that you are heading north. You get the fuck out of Dodge City. Tubes are a no-go as descriptions are probably out already. Some faces do not need describing. They are already known and mine was in this category. For all you know, there could have been serious trouble all round the ground. Police could be crawling all over the Tube stations in a mile or two radius of the ground. It was a two-mile yomp in the dark to Tower Bridge. Head down and a quick walk, trying to look as inconspicuous as possible without trying to overdo it because then you look totally conspicuous.

Cutting through the back streets I had to double back on myself to get back on the right side of the Thames. When I got to Tower Bridge, I felt safe. I did not think the Old Bill would pick me up going over the bridge. Once over the bridge you are home free, on the right side of the river, and hoping Old Bill have got their hands full where you have just come from.

It probably took over 40 minutes to get back to the pub. Better a 45-minute walk and a few pints than a one-minute Tube ride and arrest, cells, court appearances, fines and bans. Yes, give me that 45-minute walk any day of the week.

None of the boys were back in the pub before me. A couple

came back later. They had it on their toes after they had a little ruck. A few got nicked and held with details taken before being released. Maybe it was a bit of cocaine paranoia, but I'd gone from flying and on top of the world to absolute sobriety, with a feeling of self-consciousness and a need to be back in a safe zone. I felt extra happy to be back in the warmth of The Gregorian for a few pints before closing.

When the Old Bill start nicking, it is every man for himself at that stage, as everyone knows it is all about getting away from them. I did it the hard way that night. All in all, though, not a bad trip across the river. Could have been better – i.e., no Old Bill stopping us getting at Arsenal. It could have been worse, though – i.e., Old Bill nicking even more of us.

7
A TRIP DOWN THE WALWORTH ROAD

I was born in 1984. My old man was a regular down the old Den with his mates; he was from the Walworth Road. He and my mum moved to Bexleyheath just before I was born and that was where I was brought up. Following Millwall for me was not a choice – I was just brought up as a fan from birth. My first game was when I was about seven years old. I don't remember a lot about it but I do remember the old Den as a right run-down place. After that, my old man didn't really take me much. I suppose the last thing he wanted was a kid wrapped round him when he was out on the piss with his mates.

I didn't start going regular until I was about 14, with my mates from school. It started with about five of us and gradually our little firm got bigger and bigger. On a good day, if we were all out, there were eventually about 30 of us. We have always gone in the East Stand Upper when at home. And we started going to away games at 15. It is definitely the pride that makes you keep coming back to watch Millwall. Well, it certainly ain't the quality of the football. You know wherever you go in the country that you are respected and the locals always want to have a pop at you. That is all part of the fun of following

Millwall. Defending our reputation around the country. At The New Den, I have started to hear the following chant a lot: 'You're not scary anymore ...'

The away fans, of course, are tucked away in the safety of the North Stand Upper. They have put in the new walkway running from South Bermondsey station straight into the away end. We call it 'Cowards' Way'. The away fans don't come within 100 yards of us now.

My first bit of major trouble was the Wigan play-off game in 1999, fighting with them outside the ground on the wasteland by the stadium. A few fans got seriously hurt. Another hooligan joined the firm.

8

PLOUGHING INTO THE TRACTOR BOYS

It was a big day for us. It was March 1978, and we were in the quarter-finals of the FA Cup. Both the East Anglian clubs were known for liking a tear-up, unlike the 'family club' image they have today. We were drinking in the Thomas a Beckett pub on the Old Kent Road when someone came in saying there was a National Front march at New Cross. We finished our pints and quickly made our way down there. We were not going to support the march; we just wanted to have a look out of curiosity.

When we arrived at New Cross there was already a mob of Millwall hanging around. We started talking to them and discovered they had just steamed into the Socialist Workers' Party that were there to protest against the march. The NF crowd were over the moon, thinking we were there to back them. They got a big surprise when we attacked them and they didn't put up much of a fight. We did a better job than the Old Bill of sorting out the march. The Old Bill did not know what to do, so we turned on them, too. We headed back to the Old Kent Road for a drink, laughing about what had gone on. Later on, we arrived outside The Den and Ipswich were well up for it. There was fighting breaking out all over the place.

I went into the Cold Blow Lane end with my mates before the match; there was some sort of Wild West show going on. We were not really paying much attention and there was a coffin on the pitch. We were having a laugh about it saying they are obviously getting ready in case we lost. After the kick-off, some bright spark copper decided to put a group of the Ipswich firm that had arrived late into the Cold Blow Lane end. This sparked pandemonium and we attacked them. A few of them jumped on to the pitch to try and escape from us. I got hold of one of them by the scruff of the neck and was punching him in the head. Suddenly I went dizzy and started to stumble about. I looked around and one of my mates was kicking a geezer on the floor. I joined in stamping on his kidney area. He half managed to get to his feet and made a dash for it into the crowd. My mate asked, 'You all right?'

'Yeah.'

'That cunt caught you lovely from behind and your legs turned to jelly.' He was laughing.

'Don't worry, I saved you with me knuckle duster.'

Now people were all talking to each other, strangers trying to flush out any more Ipswich fans. We started watching the game. When Ipswich scored, fighting started breaking out again. Any Ipswich fan that had started celebrating was attacked.

After the game, I saw a fella that I knew. He told me after Ipswich had scored some Millwall had ransacked the food and drink hut inside the ground for ammo – bottles and tins – and launched everything into Ipswich in the seats. As we were talking, a fight started with another group of Ipswich outside. We joined in. I kicked one straight up the bollocks and he went down to his knees. I continued with some punches to the head. It was all over and I left him in trouble on the floor.

When I got back to the pub for a well-earned drink, we were

joined by others who told me that all the Ipswich coaches had been bricked. They had all been smashed to pieces outside the ground. That will teach them to beat us 6–1. A shit day for football but a fucking great day for rucks. Fighting all over the place before, during and after the game with the farmers, not to mention the NF and the police. Still a bit surprised, though, to read in the papers the next day, 'A full-scale riot occurred at the FA Cup quarter-final between Millwall and Ipswich. The violence involved bottles, iron bars and knives amongst other weapons.' Well, I already knew that.

Bobby Robson said, 'The police should have turned the flame throwers on them', and it also led to our chairman Herbert Burnige's resignation. All over a fucking good fight with the farmers. Bit of an overreaction, I thought, but then again it had been shown on *Match of the Day* and came only a few weeks after the documentary on the BBC about us Millwall hooligans. So I suppose we were hot news at the time. Also, after the documentary other firms wanted to have a go against us even more and, at the same time, our numbers swelled and maybe a few of the boys wanted to live up to this new image a bit. Still, I never thought for a minute I was involved in a full-scale riot. Newspapers do get carried away with a bit of sensational reporting; I think we all know that.

9
CRIME DOES SOMETIMES PAY

Press furore and knee-jerk reactions were nothing new after a Millwall game. Neither were crowd disturbances an invention of the Seventies. In fact, in March 1899, fans running on to the field caused the FA Cup semi-final between Liverpool and Sheffield United to be abandoned; the first half took 90 minutes to play because of all the pitch invasions. The referee didn't bring them out for the second half.

That was as nothing compared to what happened down in the valleys of South Wales in March 1912. A referee went to officiate at a game between Wattstown and Aberaman Athletic. After the game, he was attacked and died a short while later, resulting in one month's imprisonment for manslaughter for the perpetrator.

In 1920, The Den was closed after a missile was thrown and a fight occurred between the Newport County goalkeeper and a fan at the Cold Blow Lane end. One newspaper report said that the hot-headed goalie was flattened by the fan with a 'useful right hook'.

In 1934, crowd trouble closed The Den for two weeks following the visit of Bradford Park Avenue, known for their aggressive playing style, which upset the crowd. Not many crowds would have liked that, I dare say.

In 1947, more fans ran on the pitch to remonstrate with the referee during a game against Barnsley and an attempted attack on him was made on Cold Blow Lane after the game. The ground was closed and the club fined.

Still post-war, events and trouble became more frequent. It is only a guess but the fans from 1947 probably made up the angry mob of 200 Millwall fans in 1950 which ambushed the referee and linesman outside the Cold Blow Lane gates. The referee was assaulted. The ground was closed and the club fined again.

The 1960s, supposedly the decade of peace and love, saw fans enjoying more war and hate, and not always against opposing teams' players or supporters either. It was 1966, World Cup year – Queen's Park Rangers at Loftus Road. With Millwall finding ourselves 6–1 down, we turned on our own players and began throwing coins at them. The same year, somebody must have been cleaning out their allotment or turning over their cabbage patch and come across some old Second World War relics, because a hand grenade was thrown into the Brentford penalty area during a visit from the other Lions. Goalkeeper Chic Brodie picked it up, looked at the mini bomb and threw it into the net. A bloke named PC O'Connell then retrieved it, stuck it into the back pocket of his police issue trousers and took it to the local nick. Health and safety was a bit more lax in those days! It failed to explode, luckily for them and everyone else! It was confirmed as a dud, though it is likely that whoever threw it thought it was real.

The following year, the Plymouth Argyle team coach was smashed up after they ended our unbeaten 56-home-game run. Of course, there is nothing in the rule book that states: 'All defeats must be accepted with the graciousness and sporting behaviour expected and described in Rule 11 (a), section blah, blah ...'

Referee Norman Burtenshaw was attacked during one game. The club was ordered to put up fencing. But honestly, anyone who wanted to throw coins or a bottle is hardly likely to be put off by a bit off fencing are they? 'But if I throw this coin, will it get over that 5ft fence?' As was proven shortly after, when Birmingham City 'keeper Jim Herriot was hit by a missile.

All these events had only shone a faint light on Millwall. Yet the football authorities, TV, radio and newspaper journalists have all enjoyed using the club as a scapegoat ever since. Consequently, a siege mentality has developed at the club and among our fans over the years.

'No one likes us, we don't care.' What other club has a chant remotely similar?

It seems clear to me that all sides' attitudes were set in stone following a couple of major events in the Seventies. First, in 1977 the BBC chose Millwall as the club to film in the production of a *Panorama* documentary about hooliganism.

Second, and only a matter of weeks after the programme was shown to the nation, we played Ipswich Town in the FA Cup. *Match of the Day* reported that a full-scale riot ensued and the game was interrupted by all the crowd trouble. After the press furore, we were fined and banned from hosting FA Cup ties at home for two years.

Into the nation's psyche were burnt the synonyms 'Millwall' and 'hooligans'. Into ours was burnt 'victimisation'. The documentary wanted to see hooligans; we gave it to them. Many believe that a self-fulfilling prophecy occurred after these events. Millwall firms expanded and became more organised from this point on. There has been no shortage of members ever since.

We went on the rampage again through Slough town centre in 1982. Yet everything was eclipsed on 13 March 1985, at Luton Town FC. At Kenilworth Road, 50 Luton fans were injured and 31 Old Bill. The incident was raised in Parliament the next day. This was a whole new league now. They called us 'the worst of the worst'. And we accepted their claims.

'We are evil ... we are evil ... we are evil ... we are evil ...'

The press and media have continued to highlight and embellish all of our misdemeanours. Consequently, of course, since the Kenilworth Road riots, our reputation as the number-one firm has been confirmed, consolidated and enhanced by various other events. That includes Saturday, 8 November 1986, the day I 'became' a hooligan. After the fighting with Leeds, we were forced to make all home games all-ticket. The club nearly went bust because of the reduced revenue.

In 1992, Ian Wright and Nigel Winterburn were struck by coins in a League Cup game. The following year, 1993, came the Derby play-off riot with fans and police fighting. People were still invading the pitch. Old habits die hard because, in 1994, a fan was stopped from attacking Stan Collymore while he was playing for Southend at The Den.

We had a League Cup game at Chelsea in 1995. There was fighting on the pitch and outside the stadium. Then, in 1998, we were charged with and found guilty of not controlling our own fans against Manchester City. A few people ran on to the pitch. No mass pitch invasions, nothing like that.

Another play-off defeat; another riot. This time in 2000 at Wigan. Another semi-final. We rampaged through the town centre and attacked the home fans outside the ground. One Wigan fan was hospitalised after a paving slab was smashed over his head. We do not like losing in play-off semi-finals. That is official.

The next time it was in 2002 at The Den against Birmingham City. However, the two-hour riot where 70 police officers and horses received injuries was totally instigated by the baton charge by the police. Without that, it would not have happened. In 2009, in an FA Cup tie against Hull, fans rampaged through the town centre and attacked the home fans in the stadium. Later in the year came the West Ham game.

We were not the only fans to think that pitch invasions could be worth a goal or two. There was a game between Newcastle and Nottingham Forest in March 1974. A dodgy penalty and a sending off meant that 54,000 pissed off, pissed-up Geordies were not happy to see their team 3–1 down at home in the FA Cup. So 500 piled on to the pitch and charged. The referee took all the players off but not before a couple of Forest players were physically assaulted. 23 people were taken to hospital and over 100 were treated at the stadium. It took virtually ten minutes to clear the pitch and the police arrested 39 of those responsible. When the game was restarted, it appeared that the referee, linesmen and the whole of the Nottingham Forest team were all intimidated by the crowd as Newcastle scored three goals in the last 20 minutes, including, in some reports, a dodgy penalty and a clear offside. So we can safely assume some poor linesman was thinking he would have been lynched had he flagged.

And in 1974, when Newcastle fans took matters into their own hands, what did the FA do in their infinite wisdom? They annulled the game and ordered the match to be replayed on a neutral ground – Goodison Park. Why? Because 'victory was achieved in a hostile environment'. 500 fans invaded, kicking fuck out of two Forest players. The FA said, 'Replay the game please, if you would be so kind …' Imagine if that was Millwall!

Yes. That's right. I am sure that 'MILLWALL THUGS DO IT AGAIN!' or some similar headline has just popped into your head, too. And for certain Millwall would have received harsher punishment than simply 'play it again'. Words that pop into the head? Expulsion. Ban. Fine. Behind closed doors. Those type of words. Not 'play it again'. Oh no.

You're 3–1 down, and down to ten men. You run on. Attack a few of the away team, frighten the fucking life out of them and the officials, then, in the last 20 minutes, your team scores three. Including a dodgy pen. And a clear offside. You can imagine the Forest players' desperation to get off that pitch. Defeated. Eleven men against over fifty thousand – that's not very good odds. So they got the game annulled, and got their team another bite at the cherry. They got through the replay and the Geordies got to the final that year! Who said pitch invasions were useless?

10

ON THE MARCH WITH F-TROOP

I have been going to Millwall since 1960. Being a Millwall fan is all about having a good piss up, having a good punch up, having a laugh, the occasional mini success, hating West Ham, standing your ground and supporting the team.

We travelled up to Wolverhampton by train in 1975 with a tidy firm of about 100 of us. We got into the home end behind the goal and steamed into the Wolves firm. They tried to put up some resistance but were no match for our quality outfit. We took over their end. Outside the ground, we tried to get at Wolves again but they hid inside the ground. There was a burger stall that a few of the fellas picked up and tried to use as a battering ram to push the stadium doors through, but they weren't moving.

Cardiff fans took a bit of a hiding at The Den in 1976/77 when we trapped them in a corner of the ground, so our trip to Cardiff would be a lively one. The train journey was a good one with people in fine spirits and laughing about the reception we would get. There were about 150 of us. No Cardiff at the station.

On the way to the ground some Cardiff had a go but were easily seen off. There was no trouble in the ground but it was a hostile atmosphere. Outside was a different story. Cardiff had now got together a massive mob to attack us. We got outside and it kicked off straight away. Fighting broke out everywhere. As always, we stood our ground, fighting for our lives. One of our boys pulled a machete out and hit this big, black fella straight in the gut, making him slump on the floor in a heap. The fighting continued until the police moved in. We were moved back to the train station surrounded by the Old Bill while Cardiff fans continued to attack us all the way back to the station. We stood our ground.

I remember a visit from Spurs the same season when there was a load of them down the Old Kent Road. They were getting battered and tried to run away. A few Millwall jumped on the back of a geezer's horse and cart and gave chase down the road. When they caught up with them, they jumped off and battered them some more.

One of my mates had an old van that we took up to Oldham in the late Seventies – right old shit heap. About ten of us piled into it at the Elephant & Castle. We were sure it would not make the long journey to the outskirts of Manchester.

We set off across London and up the M1 with the van full of beer. After many stops on the way, we finally arrived at the ground. We got into the stadium and met up with some more Millwall who told us they had got into their home end. In the Chaddy End, they had been outnumbered ten to one and took on their firm.

At the end of the game, we pulled out of the ground. The home firm was waiting for us, about 200 of them. There were even numbers now. It was carnage, an absolute blood bath and Oldham were annihilated.

One of the funniest things I've heard at football was the petrol bomb Newcastle threw at the visiting West Ham firm.

Two West Ham got burnt and the Ice Cream Firm melted away.

It was May 1983, and we had a big relegation decider at Chesterfield. It was the usual train journey with plenty of beer. On arrival in Chesterfield, we were met by a sea of police and everyone coming off the train was subjected to a search from the boys in blue. After the coppers had touched everyone up (you can tell most of the Old Bill are closet queers the way they search you, there is no need to touch you the way they do but them uniforms and handcuffs are all a bit kinky) we were herded to the ground. Flanked by the Old Bill with them shouting orders for us to stay in the escort. We approached the ground from about a mile's walk and were met by more Old Bill. They were well prepared for us to lose and go on the rampage. We took about 3,000 to find out our fate. We outnumbered the home fans by two to one. The match was played through a heavy thunderstorm and people were looking for any sort of cover to keep the wind and the rain out.

The first half was a tight affair with not much coming in the way of chances. Then, four minutes before the break, Dean White fouled the Chesterfield captain Bill Green. It resulted in a scuffle with the ref sending off both players. In the second half, we made the breakthrough after being awarded a penalty that Dave Cusack slotted home. People were glued to their radios relaying other scores. If Chesterfield equalised, we were going down. It was a nervous last few minutes. The referee blew his whistle causing wild celebrations and a pitch invasion. Then we realised it was a false alarm. Fuck knows what the ref had blown up for but it looked to me like he had signalled the end of the game. There was still a lot of Millwall on the pitch and the police came on with dogs to restore order. A few more minutes were played and we got the result we came for.

The journey back to the station was the same as before.

Heavy handed, but we were in great spirits. The baiting of the mounted police and dog handlers continued as we were bundled on to the train. I heard the police heave a sigh of relief. George Graham had performed a miracle. Chesterfield had avoided being ransacked and we avoided relegation, too.

11

THE PRIDE OF
LONDON'S LIONS

'Millwall is more than a football club ... it is a way of life.'
Anthony Clare, speaking on the BBC's
Panorama Special (1977)

Millwall Rovers were founded by the workers of JT
Morton in Millwall in the East End of London on the
Isle of Dogs in 1885. We were one of the first clubs to form in
London. JT Morton opened their first English cannery and food
processing plant on the Isle of Dogs at the Millwall dock in
1870, and they attracted a workforce from across the whole of
the country, including the east coast of Scotland. The group of
tinsmiths who founded Millwall Rovers were predominantly
Scottish, which is why they chose blue and white for their club
colours. They were nicknamed The Dockers. Our club secretary
was 17-year-old Jasper Sexton, the son of the landlord of The
Islander Pub in Tooke Street where Millwall held their meetings.
The first chairman of the club was Irish international footballer
and local doctor William Murray-Leslie, who never actually
played for the club.

Our first fixture was in 1885 against Fillebrook, who played in Leytonstone. Our newly-formed team was well beaten 5–0, but in our first season we were only beaten three times. In November 1886, the East End Football Association was formed and, with it, came a Senior Cup competition. Millwall made it to the final against London Caledonians, with the game being played at the Leyton Cricket Ground. The match finished 2–2 and the teams shared the cup for six months each.

A sign of future success? Don't fucking think it was somehow. During that season, we even played two games on the same day, both at home. The first was a 0–0 draw against Dreadnought in the morning and the second was a 4–1 win against Westminster Swifts in the afternoon. And players today moan about three games in a week!

We went on to become founder members of the Southern League, which we won for the first two years of its existence. In those days, the Football League was in its infancy and consisted mainly of northern clubs such as Bury, Notts County, Sheffield United and Preston North End. In the south, the Southern League was not only seen as a rival league, but more prestigious. We were also the Western League Champions in 1908 and 1909.

In those early days, we would often attract 30,000–40,000 spectators to a game, especially at our second ground on North Ferry Road. Not bad given the lack of transport – 40,000 walking up the North Ferry Road. It was around this time we turned down an invitation to join the Football League, and the place was offered instead to a small club from south-east London called Woolwich Arsenal.

For the original Millwall fan, work revolved around the dock with crime and ducking and diving being an off-shoot of dock work. Men were able to get their hands on all sorts of commodities to sell or exchange on the black market. In this era and area, it was normal for young men to get involved in a life of crime. In south-east London, some of Britain's most notorious criminals were born, including the great train robbers, the Brink's-Mat and Securitas robbers, and Frankie Fraser.

Even the origins of the word 'hooligan' came from south-east London. It derives from an Irish family that terrorised Southwark in the late 1800s. Their name is variously spelt as Houlihan or Hooligan, and they came to London from Limerick. Patrick was a bouncer and a professional hard man between the 1850s–70s. He and his band of merry men – young men who wore boots with iron-toe-plated fronts – drank in the Lamb & Flag, and their life revolved around violence and criminality. The gangs were involved in robberies, pick-pocketing, stabbings, vandalism and gang fights. A widespread disregard for law and order existed in that part of London. Patrick Houlihan eventually killed a policeman and was sentenced to life in prison, where he died. Latterly, in the early twentieth century, the word 'hooliganism' was used by Arthur Conan Doyle in the Sherlock Holmes tale *The Adventure of the Six Napoleons*.

Southwark was an English Wild West with taverns, brothels and gambling dens. A very violent place where crooks and highwaymen went looking for a good time, and a refuge for criminals from the City of London. So into this backdrop was born Millwall Football Club.

The nickname The Lions came in 1900 along with the club motto, 'We fear no foe, where e'er we go', after a Cup run. In 1910, after four ground changes in and around the Isle of Dogs and to accommodate growing crowds, the club decided to move south of the River Thames to New Cross. The Den was born. This attracted new supporters from the new area, which also had a big docklands workforce in the Rotherhithe, Bermondsey and Deptford communities, continuing the theme of support from the local dockers and forming the fan base for the club's future. It also meant that we were allowed to be the only team in the country to kick off our home games at 3.15pm on a Saturday afternoon, to accommodate the late-finishing dockers.

Typical Millwall. We appeared in a Wembley final but because it was an unofficial wartime Cup Final it is not acknowledged in the record books. With the war in Europe in its last days, there was a relaxation over the number of spectators allowed to attend games. The attendance was 90,000, which is the largest crowd Millwall have ever played in front of. We were favourites to win but played poorly and lost 2–0 to Chelsea. We blamed the 'guest players' in the Millwall side who took a back-hander or two. Typical Millwall again – most of the Chelsea players ended up at the Millwall party, which apparently continued well into the early hours of the morning.

In the doldrums during the Fifties, our form was poor and we suffered relegation on a regular basis. One highlight during this period was the match we played to mark the opening of our floodlights. A crowd of 25,000 saw us beat Manchester United.

It was at The Den that crowd trouble and disturbances were first reported by the national press. By the Fifties, the newspapers were starting to report events with the hysteria that we see so frequently today. They began linking it to social problems rather than seeing it as men on a Saturday afternoon letting off a bit of steam after working all week. By the mid-Sixties, the men involved in trouble at a football match were being labelled 'hooligans'. This caused panic in the media in the build up to the 1966 World Cup, with the reports of possible trouble at the tournament. Accusations flew of English football being 'infected with the disease of hooliganism'.

Following the World Cup, which had passed without any real incident, a major report occurred in the *News of the World*. It was 1967. The report told of how Manchester United fans had brought down a large following to West Ham, determined to claim the North's first major terrace success in London. The predictable headlines from that day were no different from today's, screaming 'SOCCER'S DAY OF SHAME'.

No change there then. This victory cemented Man United's 'Red Army' as one of the country's most notorious firms in the Sixties. With the continued incidents involving Millwall throughout the Sixties and Seventies, we became without doubt the leaders of football hooliganism in the public's eyes, following firstly the BBC documentary on the club in 1977, and secondly the riot against Ipswich Town in 1978. Then came the Luton Town riot. In 1985, Millwall was in crisis – bad publicity and falling gates led to the near collapse of the club.

During the summer of 1987, the London Borough of Lewisham council leader David Sullivan sponsored Millwall for £70,000 a year for four seasons. It was the first local authority to do so, and it coincided with arguably our most successful period. After one promotion, George Graham resigned and was replaced by John Docherty, previously a manager at Brentford and Cambridge United. He didn't really float our boat but, in his second season as manager, Millwall surprised everyone and won the Second Division Championship, which got us promoted to the top flight of English football for the first time in our history. Docherty stated at the time, 'The full enormity of what we had achieved struck home that night as we celebrated with the players and fans. When Frank McLintock and I went into The Royal Archer with the Championship trophy, I think most of our fans thought that I was a cardboard cut-out! They couldn't believe that we wanted to have a drink with them and let them hold the trophy, but for me that sort of moment is what the game is all about.'

12

CHEWING TOFFEES

It was in February 1973 when we made the journey to Liverpool by train for the FA Cup fourth round tie. It was absolutely packed. Everyone had plenty of booze with them and we were well pissed by the time we got to Lime Street. We came out of the station straight into a reception committee. We were at the front fighting and more and more Millwall came streaming out of the station behind us. We must have had about 2,000 with us once out of the station, our top fighters all on the scene. We started to come off better in the exchanges. There were running battles everywhere. The police were trying to maintain order but weren't having much luck. We later found out the mob that had met us at the station was both Everton and Liverpool. They had joined together to take us on but still the two of them were not good enough to beat us. They started to back off once we got the upper hand.

We made our way to the ground; en route there were attacks from small mobs but nothing major. They would attack but run as soon as the fighting started. When we got into Goodison Park, we mobbed up near the home end, The Gwladys Street Stand. We made an attempt to get into their end. With the fighting even and Everton not giving any ground, we regrouped for another charge, and this time they ran. A few stood to fight but we kept steaming into the away end, pushing them back. We looked round and we were in their end. We had taken their end, something no other team had done.

The fighting was continuous throughout the match. It carried on outside with us once again coming out on top. There were a few small attacks on the way back to Lime Street. Later, we found out there had been a few casualties. Seven Millwall had been slashed and stabbed. But that is the risk you take fighting at football. I mean, seven slashed out of two thousand is not a bad percentage when we could claim to be the only firm to take the Everton home end.

In October 1995, we drew Everton in the second round of the League Cup, a year after beating Arsenal and Chelsea. We had nothing to fear. The game itself finished 0–0. Midweek matches at The New Den. I remember it being about three-quarters full and a good atmosphere. There were a good number of away fans considering it was a midweek, second-round League Cup game. We expected them being a top-flight team to bring a good firm. We knew their top boys were coming.

We were waiting in The Cliftonville Tavern by the ground but, instead of coming to our main pub, they went into The Barnaby. It was full of scarfers and they got themselves picked up by the Old Bill. They knew where we would be, yet they went to another pub to get a safe escort into the ground. Poor show really.

We weren't too optimistic going up to Goodison as it was advantage to Everton really having drawn the first leg away. It was another midweek match and a fair few of the boys went up.

We took 800, and 500 would have been ready for a ruck. Big jolly up on the train. It was not a football special but just a normal train with loads of regular passengers. About half the train was Millwall, all in good spirits having a drink and a laugh. A few of the regular passengers probably felt like it was a long journey; London to Lime Street and surrounded by Millwall, too. But we were well behaved. No trouble on a train like that. No opposition hooligans to fight with but a few London blues must have hidden their hats and scarves.

We arrived at Lime Street an hour or so before kick-off and walked along to Goodison, about 400 or so. There was a pretty good-humoured and non-menacing police presence that walked us at a quick pace to the ground. Bit of a surprise, really, because I was expecting a fairly unfriendly reception. Got to the ground and still no sign of any Everton fans looking for a ruck. Into the ground and the game is about to kick off. Fuck me, we went 2–0 up! No shock when they pulled it back to 2–2. Fucking shock upon shock. 4–2 Millwall, and we'd beaten one of the big boys again. Loads of banter going on with us and the home fans but there was no trouble. Game over and back to Lime Street, we all walked in great spirits. A bit disappointed that there had been no ruck but more than delighted to win. It was a late one back into London, straight on the Tube and home to bed. A good day out.

13

OUTNUMBERED ... BUT NOT OUTCLASSED

One of the funniest things that happened was at QPR's ground, Loftus Road, in March 1966. There had been no real trouble before the match and inside the ground it was a good atmosphere because both clubs were pushing for promotion from the Third Division. Until they scored. And scored again. And again. And again. We played fucking shite and QPR won 6-1 in the end.

After each goal, our now almost customary pitch invasion ensued, until a stadium announcer threatened that the game would be abandoned if we continued. Not the sharpest thing to shout over the Tannoy.

We had already turned on our own players by throwing coins at them. One hit Len Julians on the head and he picked it up and threw it back at us. After the announcement, a load of our boys invaded again in the hope of getting it abandoned and replayed. Probably around 40 of our boys sat down on the pitch and refused to move. We were all laughing and cheering them on, then Billy Gray, our manager at the time, must have been asked to help because he pleaded with them to leave the field, which they finally did. We gave them a big cheer but it didn't hide the fact that we were shit on the day and promotion was slipping away.

A couple of weeks later, we went to Oxford and clashed with them in the town centre and in the ground. We lost the game and promotion was gone.

Fast-forward two years to November 1968, and we had heard that 'Boro had been involved in a few rows, so knew they would bring a mob down. We waited around New Cross Gate station. There were about 50 of us hanging about with a few near the station entrance keeping lookout. Someone shouted they were here. As a group came out of the station entrance, we steamed straight into them. They were annihilated. They didn't even put up a fight. Any left standing made a run for it. So much for 'Boro's firm. And we kicked their arse on the pitch 2–0.

We decided to give them a second chance and, a couple of years later, we made our way to Middlesbrough on the train, about 70 proper fellows; none of the kids, just all grown men. Got off at the station and found the place to be dead, a right shit-hole. Found a pub, only a little quiet boozer and had a few pints before it was time to make our way to Ayresome Park. Once in the ground, we made our way straight into the home end. It was occupied by what would be called a 'youth firm' today. They took a hiding. We took their end.

Then in February 1972, we had an away day against the farmers. We arrived just before the game in Norwich and, when we got into the ground, it was kicking off already. We surged into the River End Stand where all their chaps used to be and had a good scrap with them. We started to get the upper hand although were only numbered about 50. We really began to give it to these Norwich fans that were standing their ground. I caught one fella with a left hook after he came at me throwing big haymakers. I managed to move back and caught him flush.

He fell straight down the terrace steps. After we had dealt with them, we moved to the Barclays Stand and about 20 of us steamed into more home fans. After announcing our arrival, we engaged in fierce fights which were eventually interrupted by the Old Bill.

Outside after the game, we were fighting the locals all the way to the station. Those farmers were fucking tough bastards.

The next year, we played Bolton. We came out of the ground, about 100 of us proper chaps. We were ready for it. Bolton came charging at us and we were well outnumbered. We got trapped with our backs to the stadium wall and Bolton in front of us. This big cunt came towards me. I kicked him straight up the bollocks and he went down rolling about. Then a tall, wiry cunt came at me swinging a lump of wood. I put my arm up and, as it hit my arm, it went numb ... then a shocking pain. I thought my arm was broken. Out of the corner of my eye, someone caught him right on the jaw and he hit the floor in a heap. I moved back into the crowd with my arm killing me. These cunts just kept on coming. We were heavily outnumbered but kept fighting them.

The Old Bill arrived, getting in between the two fighting groups and they got the situation under control straight away. A fucking mad buzz when the odds are stacked against you like that. There is always someone in front of you to fight and it is totally different to when there are more of you. In one scenario, you are trying to get involved as much as you can and, in the other, you are involved as much as you can cope with. I always preferred being outnumbered. More action. Though with my arm fucked, it was good to get back to SE4 that night as it throbbed like fuck all the way home.

14

AUNTIE PAYS
A VISIT

It was the documentary by the BBC in 1977 that really brought Millwall to people's attention. Our then manager Gordon Jago, who thought he was a clever, young football manager with revolutionary marketing ideas, decided on an idea to boost the club's profile. There hadn't been any major incidents reported in the press so he thought this was an ideal opportunity to rid the club of its bad image. What old Gordon was thinking you can only guess. This was the guy who had brought in Romark, the hypnotist, to help the players. Well, I suppose he was 'thinking outside the box'. Some of the boys suggested that if his thoughts had been *inside* the box, maybe we would have scored more and conceded less under him.

He obviously thought it was safe to get the cameras in, but it backfired on him big time. Just a few months after it was aired, Gordon Jago lost his job due to the fallout. What were you thinking, Gordon?

What was obvious was that the programme-makers were thinking along completely different lines to Gordon. The documentary attempted to explore the phenomenon of hooliganism by focusing on Millwall. Its objective was to go beyond the popular press, but it served only to reinforce the stereotypes. It set out to identify violent gangs and explore the theory widely held at the time that they were linked to extreme right-wing groups. Trying to prove and project a link between football hooliganism and National Front fascism, they filmed the F-Troop fighting at Bristol. They showed interviews with some members of the F-Troop, notably Harry the Dog, they showed National Front supporters selling literature outside the ground (something never seen before or after that day) and they also aired an interview with Martin Webster, NF's national activities organiser, all to add weight to their claims.

When the club and local police saw the final edit, they asked the BBC to scrap the programme. Sir Ian Trethowan, Director General of the BBC, refused. The documentary was aired to the nation in early 1978.

It was only a few months after the England v Scotland 1977 Home International at Wembley. After Scotland won 2–1, their supporters invaded the pitch and destroyed one of the goals. The scenes were broadcast live and it is identified as one of the key moments when football hooliganism caught the interest of the public, the press and politicians.

So why did the BBC pick Millwall? Pitch invasions, fighting, intimidation, demonstrations and missiles thrown had all been recorded from the early years. That was the image of our crowd at that time. It probably goes back to the early days. East End dockers and Millwall dockers were from a background of poverty where toughness was necessary to survive. Hard work and danger went hand in hand. This mentality and approach to life was handed down from generation to generation. All these facts went on to shape those early crowds.

The Isle of Dogs was cut off by the docks and was poor, but proud of its isolation. It saw itself as separate and different. In

1910, The Den opened across the Thames in Deptford. The new supporters from Bermondsey, Rotherhithe and Deptford all had similar backgrounds. The average attendance went from 24,000 to 47,000 in the Forties. This at a time when Millwall fans famously attacked our own directors, including a Mr Purcer, the local car dealer on the Old Kent Road. We were never afraid of voicing our anger. The volatility of our boys continued.

Like a lot of areas post-war, the Millwall area suffered. Traditional industries such as the docks were either closed down or relocated. Communities were fractured and the construction of the big tower blocks only led to further discord. A large black community moved in. Loyalty to club and community often led to contempt for outsiders and racism became widespread. Throughout the country, racist chants became a big part of football – not just at Millwall – and the intensity of the abuse probably explains why black supporters were not attracted in any great numbers at stadia throughout the country. Little was done by clubs or football authorities to challenge this behaviour for many years. Yet it does explain the BBC's angle when it came to make the programme.

Between 1927 and 1949, we were punished by the FA on six separate occasions. In March 1934, the FA closed the ground for two weeks following, as Ted Hufton from the *Sunday Pictorial* called it, 'over exuberance' at a match against Bradford. The fans had held a demonstration against the directors.

During November 1938, the club was fined after fans threw missiles and forced the players to leave the pitch. After World War II came the headline 'MORONS OF MILLWALL DO IT AGAIN'. Similar headlines were a fairly regular occurrence, especially after one referee was assaulted by over 100 fans after a game –

again The Den was closed. During the mid-Fifties, all football crowds declined as two-thirds of people now owned their own television and had found a new form of entertainment.

During the Sixties, ends at grounds with youths on terraces singing songs were properly established. The demonology of youth begins in the national press – mods, rockers, football fans and hooligans lived up to this image. A dummy hand grenade was thrown at The Den. The press were all over it: 'HAND GRENADE SHAMES SOCCER', 'DEN OF SHAME', 'SOCCER FANS ON THE RAMPAGE'.

It could be argued that the club had done everything within its power at this stage. It could also be argued that the club was paying lip service to a problem it did not really care about. We raised the entrance fees, banned some fans and issued stern warnings in match programmes during this time. After all this, referee Norman Burtonshaw was struck by fans in a widely-reported incident which finally forced the club to act and put its money where its mouth had been for a while. Consequently, in November 1967, cages went up at The Den.

By the time the BBC wanted to pick a club to base a documentary on, it's safe to say we had been in the press once or twice!

As for the *Panorama* documentary itself, although it set out to establish right-wing links to the firm, it did contain some comedy genius from the Beeb, and some of the great quotes from the F-Troop faithful broadcast in the programme stand true today, but also explain why the BBC picked Millwall.

'Millwall is more than a football club ... it's a way of life.'

'All we're going for ... is a good game of football, a good punch-up and a good piss-up and that's all about Millwall.'

As for the narrator? Quality. 'Like any other set of supporters, they cheer on their team, question the referee's parentage and exchange pleasantries with the police, who they call "the Old Bill".'

Genius! They did try to explain the structure of the firm too, though.

'At the bottom of the hierarchy are the youngsters. They call themselves The Halfway Line and, when it comes to aggro, they imitate their elders for, as they grow older, they have a clear choice to make. Some of them graduate to Treatment – they are the ones in the surgical masks, they don't start fights but they are always there when they happen. In the trench warfare of the terraces, it is F-Troop that go over the top. F-Troop are the real nutters, self-confessed loonies like Harry the Dog who go looking for fights and are seldom disappointed. Hooliganism has become a part of football folklore – this is the view of Millwall that has become familiar, building up notoriety for Harry the Dog.'

They didn't tell the viewers how they asked the boys to attack the opposing fans, or how they told us to invade the pitch because it makes good television. The surgical masks came about – or so the story goes – because one of the boys was working in St Thomas's Hospital. Apparently, he would just be grabbing big handfuls for every game. The name 'Treatment' stuck after an away trip. Some copper said to our boys, 'You lot didn't half give them some treatment.' And so the name was born.

Twelve years later and another interview was conducted. One fan in this particular film remained critical of the programme-makers' approach. He claimed they set out to paint a picture and didn't want any information other than that which was going to confirm the picture. The effect? A self-fulfilling prophecy. Pre-programme, it had just been a laugh. Get pissed and have a punch-up, no real organisation involved. Post-programme, the violence became more premeditated and organised and fans began cutting out pieces from the papers. Some wanted notoriety. The press didn't disappoint. Some gloried in the publicity and acted up to the cameras. Why not? It was 1978. The effects were not the same as they are now. No jail, bans, fines or passport confiscation then. Of course, it also meant Millwall would now continue to be singled out in coverage and in calls for punishment.

The only positive conclusion from the documentary was that it failed to establish any links with extreme right-wing groups. The programme-makers failed in their efforts to link Millwall with the National Front, quite simply because the links did not exist. One thing is for sure – we became the number-one firm and page one of the hooligans' weekly news after the documentary. And stayed there. Thank you very much, Auntie Beeb. It really may not have been possible without your help.

Efforts to associate us with right-wing racist groups did not stop there; they continued more blatantly in the national press. On 16 September 1993, Derek Beacon of the BNP won a council by-election in the Millwall ward of Tower Hamlets with a vote of 1,486 and a winning margin of 7 votes. Steven Howard, the *Sun*'s new hotshot writer, made a trip to The Den the following Saturday to report on Pat Van Den Hauwe's home début. On a mission to dig some dirt after slating Van Den Hauwe, he finished the article, 'Not long ago, chairman Reg Burr claimed that racism has been all but eliminated from Millwall. How odd then that the fascist BNP have won their first seat in Tower Hamlets last week in the Millwall ward.'

A dangerous remark as press speculation leads to police interest, which could, in turn, entice people to act out what the Old Bill are looking for. At any rate, it was a curious remark indeed. Howard had not mentioned any racist chants in his report, but still found time to mention an unrelated council by-election in another part of London. It just happened to have the same name as our football club – Millwall. But it had no relevance apart from being where the club originated 108 years before. This was a main article in the *Sun*, the best-selling paper in the country. The majority of people outside (and a few inside) London, would not know that Millwall FC were based nowhere near Millwall and would then associate the BNP with our club after reading this article. Hence, Millwall have since been labelled with this right-wing tag without any real justification. There's no more a racist problem at Millwall than at any club, and certainly no high-profile members of the firm are members. Unlike Chelsea, who have C18 links. The majority of Millwall fans these days are from south-east London and north Kent, which is definitely not East London or Tower Hamlets.

15

THE HATTERS
GO MAD

Few games have quite as many repercussions for a club as the one we played on 13 March 1985 against Luton. That game really brought things down heavy on us. And after the trouble, everyone was on to us – the club, the Old Bill, even the Government! That game caused Luton to ban all away fans for the next four seasons.

At the end of that night, we had created havoc for ten hours. On the afternoon before the game – riot. In the stadium – riot. Through the town centre after the game – riot. We were already the most notorious hooligan firm in the country by 1985, while Luton Town had their own fringe of hooligans in the MIGs (Men in Gear).

It will always be remembered as the worst case of football hooliganism in history. The trouble that night changed football for ever. Millwall, then a Division Three side, were drawn to visit First Division Luton Town. Luton had just beaten their 'arch rivals' Watford in the previous round, without incident. We had just upset the odds with a 2–0 home victory over top-flight Leicester City. On the day of the match, Luton were second-bottom of Division One and facing relegation, while we were third in Division Three and pushing for promotion. The classic league positions for an upset? How true. They had some good players – Brian Stein, Mick Harford and the big, yard dog skipper, Steve Foster – but they were not playing well at this time. So we fancied our chances. We had Fashanu, centre-back Dave Cusack and our captain Len Briley. Oh yes, we fancied our chances.

Although Luton were asked by Millwall to make the Wednesday night match all-ticket, the warning was not heeded. It was probably a disproportionately large away following; twice the size of our average home gate had arrived on the day of the game. We were talking about this game for weeks, a big game against a First Division side in the Cup.

We arrived early in the day, setting up in two pubs in Luton town centre. The local youths made one show of bravado but it was pathetic. Luton have never been known as having a decent firm and, considering they were up against the main firm in the country, they didn't stand a chance.

By 5.00pm, pubs and newsagents around the town were having their windows smashed as the police struggled to cope. The firm just ransacked the bars and shops in the town centre, and looted them. And anyone identified as a Luton fan was bashed up. The Old Bill now wanted to get us into the stadium. We made our way to the ground. There was aggro with the Old Bill all the way to Kenilworth Road.

The Kenilworth Stand was at that time still a vast terrace and always reserved for the away supporters. We were herded into it about an hour before kick-off. It was already getting really packed. People were getting crushed in little pockets and were climbing up anything to make some room. Ten minutes later, the home fans started goading us. The police were helpless as hundreds of us scaled the fences in front of the stand and rushed down the pitch towards the Luton supporters in the now packed Oak Road End. We made a serious run at them. They made a serious run away from us. A hail of bottles, cans, nails and coins saw them fleeing up the terraces. Their numbers were still growing as more fans entered the stands, which meant that there was little they could do to avoid the missiles. As this went on, more Millwall started coming into the away end. It was overflowing by 7.00pm – 45 minutes before kick-off – with spectators even perched on the scoreboard. The turnstiles had been broken down.

The official attendance on the night was 17,470. Luton had estimated we would bring 3,000. We had actually brought 10,000. That is the thing with Millwall; for average games, we have shit crowds but for big games we get big numbers. The bulk of the estimated 10,000 Millwall fans that gained entrance to the stands that night were loud, hostile and volatile.

Now it was getting dangerous. More spilled on to the pitch behind the goal and we ran into the Bobbers Stand where a group of Luton were. Again they ran. The Old Bill were trying to push us back into the away end, which had also filled up even more. Instead we ran into the Main Stand where Luton had mobbed up. This time they tried to stand and fight but were overrun. Those that stood took a right beating. A few then turned and ran and it was not long before the rest of them followed, a couple dripping in claret.

The players came out to warm up and almost immediately vanished back up the tunnel. Some of us then set upon the Bobbers Stand. We began ripping out seats and brandishing them as weapons – paying no heed to the notice on the electronic scoreboard stating that the match would not start until we returned to our allocated area. An appeal from our manager George Graham over the ground's loudspeaker was also ignored. It was only when he appeared on the sidelines that we finally returned to the Kenilworth Stand. Even after this, a noticeable number of our boys had managed to infiltrate the Main Stand and were involved in fights. More seats were ripped out. The arrival of police dogs helped to clear the pitch in an attempt to get the match to begin on time. Many were watching events from on top of the Bobbers Stand after climbing the floodlight pylons. The match started after we returned to the away end, which by now was dangerously overflowing.

Luton started the match kicking towards our supporters. After only 14 minutes, the game was halted as we began to riot again. After 15 minutes, we invaded the pitch. We were having running battles with the police. This went on for almost half-an-hour before calm was restored. The referee took both teams off for 25 minutes before bringing them back on to complete the half.

Brian Stein put Luton ahead on 31 minutes and they led by this score at half time. Luton continued to lead as the match entered its final stages; they probably feared that the pitch invasions were now being staged in order to have the tie abandoned and therefore prevent a Millwall defeat. They were right. We attempted to disrupt the match but extra police managed to keep control. There were a few more minor disturbances. Some seats were ripped out and one of these hit a steward in the head. Luton goalkeeper Les Sealey, who stood in front of the Millwall fans in the second half, was hit on the head by a missile. They also found a knife in the goalmouth after the game.

Luton won 1–0 and that was enough for us; we invaded the pitch. Both Luton and Millwall players sprinted to the dressing room as fast as they could. One Millwall rushed towards Luton coach Trevor Hartley and tried to grab him. He wriggled free and raced towards the tunnel after the players. We made for the Bobbers Stand again and started to rip out seats as fences were torn down. The seats were thrown on to the pitch at the police. They fell back, regrouped, then charged in waves, batons drawn.

Gradually the police forced us back. We then started to rip seats from the Main Stand and threw them at them – 'makeshift plastic spears' said one report. The police had some serious casualties. Of the 81 people injured, 31 were policemen. One, a sergeant named Colin Cook, was caught in the centre circle and hit on the head by a concrete block. He stopped breathing but another resuscitated him while being punched, kicked and hit by the same concrete block. We are evil.

The back and forth continued for some time. More seats were being ripped out behind us and thrown on to the pitch; we were picking them up and launching them at the Old Bill, who were pushed back to the end of the pitch. There was a baton charge. We moved back to the Main Stand again, ripping out even more seats as missiles. Finally, we left the ground, moved to outside the stadium and rampaged through Luton, devastating anything in our way. The carnage continued as a three-way battle between us, MIGs and the police developed. Smashed cars, shops and homes were left in our wake.

When the police finally brought it under control, 31 were arrested and taken to Luton Magistrates' Court the next morning. Our boys took the piss in the court and the majority of them identified themselves as supporters of teams other than Millwall – Chelsea and West Ham included. This led, of course, to claims over the years that on this day our Millwall mob was made up from the élite of other top firms from London.

Now let us just stop and think about this for a minute. Why would Millwall even want to round up a firm including these other clubs, let alone to take on little Luton, a club that can only get excited when they play Watford? Plus, how would all these other clubs feel about being together? Total bollocks! There is no doubt we have fans from outside London. That is fine by me. We know all hooligans wish they were Millwall fans anyway. Maybe the outsiders that run with us have a soft spot for the club. Maybe they just want a bit of trouble and use Millwall as the vehicle. But to suggest there is any organisation or recruitment of any other firm is utter bullshit. Different sets of fans cannot even get on at an England game, let alone them coming to Millwall. I heard Stoke had a tear-up with Burnley, and Chelsea and West Ham are never going to mix at an England game. This claim that Millwall use other clubs to swell their numbers is an urban myth. Mainly used by firms taking a hiding. This was Millwall boys having a laugh! And this was how the urban myth developed. Millwall use other firms! Bollocks. Utter fucking bollocks. That was a bad night for Luton. Their town was ransacked; their firm humiliated.

So what happened in the aftermath? Luton manager David Pleat was left 'feeling empty'. And I followed their results after that night; they got beaten by Everton 2–1 in the semi-final, and we won promotion to the Second Division six weeks later.

Luton Town chairman, Conservative MP David Evans, reacted by imposing a ban on all away supporters from Kenilworth Road from the start of the 1986/87 season, as well as introducing a scheme that would require even home supporters to carry membership cards to be admitted to matches. Margaret Thatcher's Conservative Government also set up a 'war cabinet' to combat football hooliganism. They attempted to have membership schemes based on the Evans model adopted nationwide. It even led to Chelsea chairman Ken Bates claiming he intended to erect electric fences at

Stamford Bridge to avert such an incident at his club. Nice one, Ken!

Naturally, the FA commissioned an inquiry. It concluded that it was 'not satisfied that Millwall FC took all reasonable precautions in accordance with the requirements of FA rule 31 (A) (II)'. The club received a £7,500 fine, although this was withdrawn on appeal. The penalty that Millwall faced according to most reports was that the club's name was now synonymous with all that was bad in football and society. Like that wasn't the case before. Luton Town was ordered to construct fences around its ground, a decision that was also reversed.

Shortly afterwards, Luton announced a million-pound overhaul of Kenilworth Road. They spent £350,000 on a new artificial pitch that summer and £650,000 on converting the ground to an all-seater. Funny thing was, work on the stands began in the summer of 1986 but was not finished until 2005. Twenty years after the riot, they finished the stands! Twenty fucking years!

The first match of the identity card scheme came on 26 August 1986, a First Division match against Southampton. The Football League insisted that Luton relaxed the ban for League Cup matches. Evans refused. Cardiff City fans were not allowed to visit Kenilworth Road for their second-round tie, and the club was thrown out of the competition. Fucking mad to think the actions and repercussions of that night had such far-reaching consequences. The FA announced that Luton would be allowed to maintain their ban on visiting supporters in the FA Cup. They would also allow other clubs to ban away support from Luton. Luton eased the ban. Slightly. Five hundred tickets would be given to certain clubs. This number would be doubled should the match pass without incident. The ban continued for four seasons. It was a success! No shit! Not one arrest was made, either inside or outside the ground during its enforcement. Despite this and the support of Bedfordshire Police for the scheme, Luton Town repealed the ban before the start of the 1990/91 season. The repercussions were felt for some time by plenty of people.

God alone knows what Sir Bobby Robson said about us on that night. But if he was happy for the flamethrowers to be turned on us after the Ipswich game, then only spraying us with an AK-47 would have satisfied him after the Luton riot. Millwall went from notorious on a national level, to internationally infamous. In one day.

The following day began the clean-up operation of Luton. Newspapers and television showed a lot of pictures of the stadium – surrounding streets, town centre shops and bars. It looked ... well, it looked like a riot had been raging like a tornado for hours and hours. Our reputation was set in stone.

16
HIBS SCOTCHED

It was only a pre-season friendly against Hibernian, albeit one of Scotland's top firms, but we didn't expect anything that day in August 1990. I'd gone straight to the game but one of the lads was drinking an hour before the game with 20 Millwall in The Crown and Anchor pub on the corner of New Cross and Avonley Road. Suddenly about 150 of the Hibs' firm came running towards the pub. There were a few exchanges outside and the 20 Millwall stood and tried to fight but, vastly outnumbered, they were forced inside the pub. Most of the windows in the pub were put through but, amazingly, they managed to hold off Hibs for five minutes, despite being outnumbered almost eight to one. Missiles were going back and forth – glasses, bottles, ashtrays, anything people could get their hands on. But the 150 Hibs boys did not take over the pub. They had smashed the windows but they didn't even get in the pub, let alone take it over. Good effort by our outnumbered 20 boys.

After the five-minute battle, Hibs made their way down the Old Kent Road and the Millwall from the pub chased after them. Armed with anything to hand, including bottles and bar stools, the fighting went to and fro with neither side making any ground. The 20 of our boys had all stood up to be counted to a man.

Hibs came under another hail of missiles and with the arrival of the Old Bill to restore order, they probably thought they'd had their fun for the day. It was only just starting!

When they arrived at The Den, we attacked from all sides. They ran into the ground to seek safety. After the game, their 150 being escorted to the station were stalked by 500 Millwall. On Ilderton Road, we attacked them. Everyone had heard during the match about what had happened before. Phone calls were made and people who had not been to the game were outside. These were the days before we all had mobiles, so the boys were running into pubs and phone boxes to make calls. Chaps sat in the house on a quiet, pre-season Friday evening were getting calls telling them about what happened and making their way to the ground. Others who had been having a drink in some pub around the ground, with no intention of going to the game, heard the Hibs boys were in town. All told, we had rounded up about 500. All ready for pay back.

We got to them at New Cross. It wasn't 500 mobbed up, we were scattered all over the place. Hibs were scattered, too; no massive police presence. One Hibs lad was taking a kicking and pleading with a copper, 'Help me, help me ...' The copper just ignored him; turned away and left him to us. That copper did not want to be a hero. A bit of quiet, pre-season Friday night overtime. Long before the time of the sophisticated police communication system of today. No Scottish Transport Police warning ahead of 150 Hibs fans coming down and telling the Old Bill to be prepared. He was on his own. And he did fuck all as this Hibs boy took a kicking.

There were probably about 40 of us and Hibs seemed to be

running everywhere. The first one I caught was with a big left hook. Fear does funny things to people. You can kick fuck out of someone and punch someone hard, but pure fear and his animal survival instincts kick in. Fight or flight. They get up and run. Fear means flight. Flight means run. Hibs were running.

There was another group of about ten of them at the station. We got in a few more digs but they were only interested in running now. Not necessarily into the station, they were just running anywhere, out of the range of Millwall punches and kicks. By now they had all disappeared. One of the boys told us a Hibs lad had been thrown through a shop window.

We were all milling about for a short while. They had put a few of our windows in at The Crown and Anchor and we had put a few of their heads through the windows. Pre-season friendly, eh! Everyone went back to what they were doing before the Hibs excitement and we headed up to The Foresters for a right good drink. Stayed there all night with a load of the boys and we had a good laugh about the evening's events. They had taken a liberty and ended up paying for it. I think Hibs were happy they were not in the English league facing us regularly.

17

1985 – THE YEAR FOOTBALL LIVED DANGEROUSLY

Within the space of three months in 1985, we had the Luton Town riots, Bradford and Heysel. I remember sitting in the front room watching all these events unfold on the television. Bradford – what a tragedy. A rogue cigarette in the old wooden stands. Then Heysel. On Wednesday, 29 May 1985, 39 people died and more than 400 were injured at the stadium in Brussels before the European Cup Final between Liverpool and Juventus. It didn't stop the game; it went ahead and Juventus won 1–0.

I was a Millwall fan just sitting on the floor in our front room on the Aylesbury Estate. My father was watching in disgust at rioting, fires and fatalities. I had no real inkling of the scale, import and impact of all these events unfolding. I was firmly under the impression that attending football matches was a dangerous pastime. But as an 11-year-old kid growing up in south-east London, danger to me was fascinating, intriguing, an everyday occurrence. I already knew through drinking in local pubs that football and danger went hand in hand. Even after these events, I was in no way put off from going again. If anything, attending football matches was more captivating than ever.

It was an unprecedented year in football. The Football Association banned all English clubs from playing in Europe following the events at the Heysel Stadium. Football went all political. Prime Minister Margaret Thatcher supported the ban as it was announced by FA officials outside 10 Downing Street. She called for tougher sentences on convicted football hooligans, saying, 'We have to get the game cleaned up from this hooliganism at home and then perhaps we shall be able to go overseas again.'

I was sat there wondering how they were going to come into our pub and tell all the chaps that there was to be no more fighting. That was going to be a tough job for someone. The ban affected Everton, Manchester United, Liverpool, Norwich, Tottenham Hotspur and Southampton. They were all due to compete in Europe the following season. FA secretary Mr Ted Croker said, 'It is now up to English Football to put its house in order.'

Then FA Chairman Burt Millichip acknowledged that the ban was a pre-emptive move and that UEFA (The Union of European Football Associations) would have imposed it anyway. He said it was the most difficult decision he had ever had to take, but 'it was very important that the FA took positive action and immediately'.

Politicians were now jumping in. Neil Kinnock, leader of the Labour opposition, said, 'The ban on English teams would only benefit those who caused the murderous riot in Belgium.'

The Football League, which was not consulted, was opposed to the decision. The Belgian Government had already instantly banned all British clubs from its territory until further notice. Liverpool FC, whose fans were blamed for much of the violence, had already decided to pull out of the following season's UEFA Cup competition before the FA announcement. Bradford, Luton and now Heysel, all in a matter of weeks. My head was fucking spinning as to the possibilities and dangers of going back to The Den in August.

18

DERBY FAILS TO SCALE
THE 'WALL

Millwall finished in third position in May 1994, safely making the play-offs and with a chance of getting into the Premiership. The team had been playing well all season but had no chance of automatic promotion at the end. But we were confident against a Derby side that had finished way below us, in sixth place.

We got the train up to Derby and had a right good old drink on board. The train was full, with our allocation sold out – we were all in high spirits and thinking about the Premier League. The away leg went without any incidents. No sign of the Derby Lunatic Fringe. We performed really badly and lost 2–0. In fact, we played fucking terribly and were never in the game but never thought it was all over. We could get them back to our place and turn this round.

On the day of the return leg, a few Derby were attacked at Surrey Quays station and took a bit of a hiding. Nothing else happened before the game with everyone too concerned about the match itself. We were having a few beers in The Barnaby with most people trying to be positive.

Twenty minutes gone and we found ourselves 2–0 down, 4–0

on aggregate. This was too much for Millwall fans. It was too much for me. We decided to try and get the game abandoned. It was not like there were any big conferences going on in the stands. We were in the East Lower Stand and saw a couple of people head on to the pitch. A few others also saw them and headed on, too. Someone else spotted them from across the pitch and they made a dash for it. That's how a pitch invasion happens. Everyone knows that the hope is to get the game abandoned. It was certainly my hope as I jumped over the knee-high barrier. What a way to end the first season at The New Den. Quality. Let's get this shite abandoned! The first pitch invasion lasted only a few minutes before the police and stewards herded and chased everyone back to their seats. A few stewards had tried to stop people in the first place ... sort of. Stewards are for telling people where their seat is, where to have a piss and where to get a pie. They are not going to be heroes on a day like this. They don't even have to tell people where to sit at Millwall, it has always been buy a ticket and sit wherever you like; that is what most of us had always done.

I was shunted off the pitch and headed back to the East Lower. There were a couple of new faces that had obviously been sat elsewhere before the pitch invasion and then herded into the side I was on. Everyone around the ground knew that was not the end of the matter. The atmosphere was boiling over.

The game was done and dusted and it was inevitable it was going to explode again. Towards the end of the match, it went off again. People were on the pitch. They wanted it all over. And how, because this time the playing surface was covered with 'Wall. One took a swipe at the Derby 'keeper, Taylor. He took a punch to the gut before getting down the tunnel.

When a pitch is completely covered like that there must be thousands milling around on it. Loads, just running around and jumping about. A fucking good laugh if the truth be told. All the players had been taken off, or there were certainly none to be seen in the sea of Millwall in my eyes. It didn't last for ages. Horses galore. No one wants to get in the way of one of those rampaging beasts and no one wants to get nicked. So the Old Bill restored order and the players came back out. The game was restarted and the last few minutes were played out. Uneventful. Deflated. Dejected. The dream of the Premiership shattered. It finished 3–1 to Derby, 5–1 on aggregate; 5-fucking-1 and without a fight from Millwall on the pitch. Not the Millwall way at all. Could I even be arsed to get to the Derby fans? The fight, stuffing and wind had been knocked out of me for now.

A few of us left just before the end and we headed straight for The Barnaby. The pub was empty as everybody was still in the ground. The only good thing about the whole day was having the bar to ourselves for a while. It soon filled up with many unhappy Millwall faces and we stayed until last knockings. Some of the boys tried to get to the Derby fans. The Old Bill had them well protected once again. No sign of Derby's Lunatic Fringe in the main car park. A BBC outside location van was smashed up but, after realising the Old Bill would not let them at Derby that night, it fizzled out. Everyone went home completely gutted.

We had dared to dream again with Millwall and believed the hype about the ground move taking us forward. Should have fucking known better. The next day in the papers, we were naturally front and back news: 'MILLWALL INVADE THE PITCH', 'MILLWALL HOOLIGAN TAKES A SWIPE AT THE KEEPER'.

Could not give a shite, me; we were out of the play-offs. Write what the fuck they like about the crowd. We were not getting back to the top flight of English football. And that hurt me a lot more than the swipe at the 'keeper would have hurt him. The first season at The New Den was over.

19

MAGGIE THATCHER, FOOTBALL SNATCHER

The two crowd disasters in 1985 became a watershed. A terrace surge had been the immediate cause of the deaths of 39 Italian supporters. Liverpool fans were roundly condemned for retaliating and charging back at the fans from Juventus. Yet several other contributory factors were unquestionably overlooked in the rush to blame them. Not least the woefully decrepit state of the stadium, the badly mismanaged distribution of tickets and, of course, provocation.

A month before Heysel, a fire in a wooden stand at Bradford City caused 56 deaths. The fire highlighted what thousands of football spectators had known for years – many grounds in the UK (and clearly also abroad) had been allowed to decay to the point that they had become death traps. They were all tatty monuments to the complacency of the game's authorities. The bigwigs sat in the directors' box in relative comfort and with leg room. They just had to lean over to light their Kind Eddy off the nearest person before they popped down to the lounge and free bar at half time for a stiff tot of whisky. Spectators were expected to tolerate the sub-standard facilities – which we did. A few toilets for a few thousand fans ... cold (supposedly hot) pies ... crumbling terraces and all behind cages, with little to no protection from the elements. And check any old ground, the best roof is always the one covering that director's box – fuck the peasants, let the rain come down on them.

The post-Heysel resolve to do something about football hooliganism led to some pathetic and woefully misconceived plans. No mention of upgrading the facilities, ensuring all grounds are safe for the spectators; no ensuring clubs stop overfilling grounds to critical levels for the extra revenue and then fake attendance figures for tax reasons; no new health and safety legislation that all clubs must conform to, guaranteeing the welfare of the fans.

So what did they recommend? The worst recommendation was to require spectators to produce ID cards to gain admission. ID cards? So a hooligan has got his picture on a card. So fucking what? We've got it on our passport and on our driving licences, too. Will it stop two boys from opposing firms kicking fuck out of each other?

'You wanna toe-to-toe?'

'Yes.'

'Hang on, have you got an ID card?'

'Yes.'

'OK, no fighting with you then!'

This after a season in which 56 people died at Valley Parade, Bradford, 39 in Heysel and, of course, after the Luton riot. Honestly now, do we believe that an identity card in the pocket of anyone involved in any of these events would have changed the course of history? ID cards were never going to wash in an era when we genuinely had civil liberties. Unlike today, of course – but then, we actually had freedom of speech, freedom of movement, freedom of association and innocent until proven guilty.

Luton chairman David Evans – incidentally a nearby Conservative MP – had introduced his prototype scheme that barred all away supporters from their games. The kick-off over Luton's actions did not deter the Government, whose Football Spectators' Act of 1989 made ID cards compulsory. The plan was quietly abandoned after the death of 96 fans at the Hillsborough disaster later in the same year. The ensuing report by Lord Justice Taylor held the police's crowd control methods largely to blame for the loss of life. So ID cards were not the solution to hooliganism, decrepit stadia or bad policing, and nor are they today.

But the funniest of course was 'rationalisation'. Fucking rationalisation. Old Maggie, bless her, given her love, knowledge, participation and all-round interest in our national sport, her answer was thus: the problem is too many clubs. Too many clubs equals too many opposing fans wanting to fight. Ergo – clubs should amalgamate or be swallowed up by their nearest big rival. That way there would be less opposition and rivalry and thus less fighting. Honestly, that was the solution … fuck off, Maggie!

It showed her deep-rooted disdain for football, its fans, their clubs, communities and heritage. Combined, of course, with her complete arrogance when faced with opposition to her master plan. OK, Maggie, I know you struggle to understand any opposition. As to rationalisation, let me explain. If I was to say Oxford and Cambridge must join together from tomorrow to cut out that fierce competition they have, what say you?

'Never. Outrage. Tradition. History. Generations. Impossible. We shall fight it on the beaches and in the seas and oceans. No, no, no … This lady is not for turning.'

OK, Maggie. I hear your passion. I like it. A bit similar to what football fans think of rationalisation. Now you get the fucking picture. Rationalisation? You could just imagine Luton Town Football Club chairman and Tory MP David Evans being thrilled by that one. You can just see David whispering in Maggie's ear, 'But, PM, that would for sure mean my club … '

'Who are they again, David?'

'Luton, ma'am … that would mean us being swallowed up by the new team … Greater London and surrounding areas up to the Watford Gap FC.'

'That's right, David, now get off your knees.'

'But … but … PM, mine is the only club that has followed your orders and introduced ID cards and I've also banned all away supporters.'

Having said that, given he had already proven his willingness and eagerness to kowtow to the cow, maybe we could have expected: 'Excellent idea, PM. In fact, PM … why does not one consider this, your excellentness? If we have North Counties FC, East Counties FC, South Counties FC and West Counties FC, we could have a round-robin tournament held in one week at Wembley … six games in all every year … we could cordon off the ground with tanks, cruise missiles and 30,000 troops, play the games behind closed doors at night, no TV cameras or reporting allowed and, in effect, eliminate football, ma'am.'

'Excellent idea … implement today … '

So we must stamp out a jolly good old punch-up … from the woman who gave us the Brixton riots, Poll Tax riots, the Falklands, miners' strikes, Iraq, plus rational-fucking-isation.

Any wonder we carried on being hooligans? Rationalisation! I can imagine the MPs saying, 'Not sure this one will fly, PM …'

'Well, give it wings … before I bop you on the nose.'

Only kidding, Maggie. No matter what you did or didn't do,

nothing changed the fact I was a Millwall hooligan and I fucking loved it.

What if we put countries in place of football clubs and have the same conversation? Ready? Here we go. There's too much fighting between too many countries. Let's rationalise. So big countries, like the USA, the UK and Germany all swallow up small countries. Take them over. Now everyone has to fly our flag and sing our anthem. Remind you of anything?

These attempts by the Government to police the game came after the series of events in the Eighties that culminated in Hillsborough. Our esteemed PM thought ID cards would eliminate hooliganism and that there were too many football clubs. Genius. Fucking true genius. The brains behind that one ran our country.

Of course, to her it was 'that wretched game', an unwanted irritant that she did not understand and cared even less about. Working-class entertainment that was unpredictable and dangerous. To Margaret Thatcher's Conservative Government, football and its fans were a mystery she wanted to eliminate, posing much the same threat as miners, dockers and all militant trade unionists. But at least Thatcher was honest. She fucking hated it and virtually said as much.

Everyone understands that the politicians of today love to seize any opportunity to associate themselves with football – FA Cup Finals, European Cup Finals and World Cup tournaments can always guarantee a good turnout of good old British MPs wearing scarves and pretending they know the words to songs.

Years of boardroom greed, FA incompetence and the series of disasters had brought English football to its lowest point ever. Fewer people were actually attending games than ever before. Gruesome and almost daily press reports of 'violent fans rampaging wildly' probably left anyone who did not go the match thinking that attending a game was a near life-threatening situation and that football grounds were dripping with drunk, stone-throwing, seat-ripping lunatics.

The favourite saying of the 1980s Conservative Government was that football had become a 'law and order issue'. Maybe that was Thatcher's plan. Have the Tory-controlled press paint the bleakest of pictures and kill football off that way. If that was the plan, it nearly worked. Still no one then could have foreseen football's wholesale revival during the Nineties, fuelled in the main by the income from satellite television and most notably (ironically) from a network owned by one of Thatcher's most ardent admirers.

20

MANCHESTER BEATEN RED AND BLUE

It was December 1987, and we were in the Cold Blow Lane end when our spotters shouted that there were some Man City by the away end. We had it on our toes, got there a bit lively and steamed in giving them a good hiding. There were a couple on the floor getting a right kicking when the Old Bill turned up, saving them. They were quickly put safely into the away end for the rest of the match, which we lost 1–0.

Four years later, we knew they would be coming into London Bridge and there was a tidy firm of us ready. As their Tube pulled in, we steamed into the carriage and gave them a good hiding. They put up a good fight but were no match for us. In the end, we fucked off with them beaten on the train.

And as for the red half of Manchester, it's worth thinking back to when they weren't quite the force they are now. In August 1974, we made a trip to United, who had been relegated to the Second Division. It was going to be a good day out. United had run West Ham ragged a few years before. They took over the East End of London, something they could not manage to do on their trip to south-east London.

On the way up to Manchester, I knew we had a top firm out. A few cockney Reds were sussed out on the train, battered and slung off at the next station. When we arrived at Piccadilly, some more cockney Reds came out of the woodwork; they were dealt with just as quick as the ones before.

With the Mancs having a reception outside, the Old Bill wouldn't let us out of the station. They put us back on the train to London – we were gutted. All that way to bash up some United fans from down south. We could have stayed at home and done that. To make it worse, they battered us 4–0.

It was all set for The Den. After their West Ham exploits, we were sure they would have a go, especially after we had gone to their place with a firm but could not get out of the station. Nothing. Not even a token effort. No red devils to be found anywhere outside. What a fucking major let down. Inside, a few showed themselves and soon wished they had not after being carried out on stretchers. What happened to all those cockney Reds? They could go all the way to Manchester but could not travel a few miles to The Den. They'd had enough time to recover from their beating in Manchester and on the train, so no excuses. A dull night. And the bastards beat us 1–0.

Then in January 2002, there was a real treat in store – the chance to have a tear-up with City and United on the same day! We'd made the trip to City for what was going to be the clash of the season, with them having the biggest support in the League. We knew we would get a hostile reception. A plan had been pre-arranged for us to get off at Stockport station and find a pub there, so as not to get caught in a police escort in Manchester. When we arrived at the station in London, I looked around before boarding the train. Fucking hell. This was a good turnout. There must have been 500, all chaps, all ready for a tear-up on their way to Manchester.

On the way up, everyone was in a good mood, looking forward to mixing it with Manchester's finest. Word spread through the train that there had been a meeting arranged with United who would be leaving Manchester to come and meet us. What a bonus, City and United in one day. We arrived at Stockport and, as we came out of the station, we found a pub at the top of the road. We walked in and the landlord did not know whether to laugh or cry. Within minutes his pub was packed and his tills doing overtime.

On the other hand, his pub was packed with hooligans. Worse than that. Millwall hooligans. It was a hot day so we were outside the pub when we had the call to say United were on their way. We did not have to wait long. We could see the entrance of the station from outside the pub at the top of the slope that ran down into the station. They came streaming out of the station, loads of them. We held our position outside the pub until they got about half way. Then we attacked, running at them down the hill. As we got closer, Man Utd stopped running up the hill and turned and started to run down in the opposite direction. We began to run faster. There was no way they were going to get away without any punches thrown. I caught up with one and stuck a foot out to trip him up; he fell under my feet. I stamped on him. Then carried on running while others were kicking him at the bottom of the hill. The United fans were pushing each other out of the way to get into the station. I caught one on the back of the head with a punch. The Old Bill arrived causing us to back off and saving many red Mancs from damage. No point in getting nicked; we still had City to deal with.

We were now under a heavy police escort. This was the start of a day where they would shadow us at all times. We moved off heading for Manchester Piccadilly. When we arrived, the Old

Bill cavalry and reinforcements joined. We were now completely penned in outside the station by lines of riot police, dogs, vans and a helicopter overhead. They kept us there until all our trains had arrived with the rest of the fans. We tried to break out from the escort but there was nowhere to go; the police lines were three deep.

We moved off from the station and by now there were 1,250 of us. This must have been one of Manchester's biggest ever police operations because this 1,250 were not your average football fans; this was a mob ready for a fight. I do not think there was a team in the country that could pull together a firm this big that was full of proper headcases.

The walk to the ground was a long one. I suppose they thought they would walk all the way to try and take the fight out of us. They must have forgotten they were dealing with Millwall. Scuffles started to break out with us trying to get out of the escort. This carried on for the three or so miles to the ground. When we reached the ground, a mob of City appeared making the Old Bill get a bit twitchy. We surged towards them trying to get through the police again. Now scuffles started with City but their firm moved away not fancying it.

We were put in a corner of Maine Road on to a temporary scaffold stand which joined on to a stand behind the goal. We were separated by Old Bill. Missiles started raining down on us, which we returned. Then seats were thrown by Millwall. A few of us got through the police lines and started fighting with City. It was quickly broken up by the police with us having come out on top and the Old Bill soon had it under control. They scored two in the last ten minutes after having Benarbia sent off in the first ten minutes.

After the game, we were let out of the stadium and, once outside, we were again in an escort all the way to the station. As our mob was walking through Moss Side, the locals started to come out, groups of lads throwing bottles and stones but not daring to come near us. Any time we rushed towards them, they would run. Big bad Moss Side did not want to know. A fun day out, though, with two firms in one day.

21

AGONY AND ECSTASY

We had a good start to the 1988/89 First Division campaign, topping the league on 1 October having played six games. We'd won four and drawn two and we were rarely out of the top five before Christmas. This was mainly due to our deadly duo of Tony Cascarino and Teddy Sheringham, and my hero, Terry Hurlock, who totally dominated the Millwall midfield. He was a no-nonsense, typical Millwall player.

Cascarino was signed from Gillingham for £225,000. Sheringham began his professional career at Millwall in 1982 at the age of 16, after impressing a scout when playing for Leyton and Ilford during a youth team game against us. The first live television transmission of a Millwall game was on 22 January 1989. The TV cameras picked out a banner bearing the slogan: 'It's Taken You Long Enough To Find The Den!' Well, we had only been there 79 years by then. Our first top division season ended with a tenth-place finish, which was the lowest place we had occupied all season. We then briefly led the league for one night in September 1989 after beating Coventry 4–1, but won only two more games all season and were relegated in bottom place at the end of the campaign.

The season finished on Saturday, 13 May and, in the last game, we played Southampton in a 1-1 draw. There was no trouble. The last few weeks of that season were played out under the cloud of the Hillsborough disaster. I was 16 years of age and I had been out of school for nearly three years, working on building sites earning my wage. I had been going to The Den for over ten years at this stage. I had been involved in the hardcore violence for over three years. I had been drinking in the pubs and clubs for over five years.

I thought I knew football. Like everybody else I was shocked by how so many people lost their lives on that day. Then thoughts started popping into my head: how we were treated. We were herded like animals and put into pens, thousands and thousands of us herded in and out of little cages like pigs. And those pens were too small. Many, many times those pens were too small for us Millwall fans, let alone for big clubs on FA Cup semi-final day.

The newspapers were filled with stories and tales of the Liverpool fans' behaviour. I read them all, little realising the bullshit that papers could/have/did and will continue to write. We all should know today – of course, it was one fucking big cover-up from the start. Old Bill, authorities, FA, press, everyone was quick to point the finger at fans.

What a shining example of the establishment's utter fucking contempt and disdain for football fans. That was an accident waiting to happen. Warning signs and red lights had been going off for years. To add insult to injury, cops that were working that day started to receive massive payouts, claiming to be mentally scarred and troubled. The Chief Super was quickly pensioned off aged about 48, for fuck's sake. Meanwhile, the families suffered. And still do. Justice for the 96.

I am not saying it felt like I was finished with football, but –

we went for a piss-up, a punch-up and accepted being treated like animals in the hope of a good game of football. In shitty conditions, with shitty toilets on shitty terraces. No one ever thought they would see people die going to a game of football. No one ever wanted to see people die going to a game of football. Certainly no one I ever spoke with. I was questioning my involvement with football as a whole, let alone hooliganism. This was the summer of 1989. Then something happened. Somebody gave me a tablet. An Ecstasy tablet.

I didn't know what to expect. All that I was told was, 'This is going to blow your fucking head off.'

Wow! Wow! Fucking wow! Drugs at that stage had not been such a big factor for me. Well, that changed. Oh, that changed. Overnight. Anyone who had Ecstasy in 1989 knows all about that first rush. It did exactly what it said on the tin. It blew my fucking head off. I could not control it. I was gone. In the laps of the Ecstasy gods. They lifted me up high and played around with me for about seven or eight hours. Finally, they dropped me down in a heap when they were finished with me and then dared me not to join them again. Oh, I joined them again. I'd been dared. I joined them regular. It wasn't called 'Ecstasy' for nothing.

I had no control over that first tablet. After that, well, after a few, I learnt to control that big rush. A bit. You couldn't walk. It told you when to sit down. You knew it was coming. The 15–20 minutes from when you dropped it were filled with a tingling, and knowledge of what was imminent and the slight foreboding, too. This was powerful shit and I was still not 100 per cent au fait with it.

Identical, really, to when I first started going to the match. The adrenalin rush, the slight sense of foreboding and the concern over the unexpected. Oh yes. I had replaced one powerful drug – football hooliganism – with another new, more powerful drug – Ecstasy. And what a difference it made. And not just to me. For loads. How? Well, the beer-fuelled battles were out. Nightclubs that had resembled battlegrounds with blood and guts and ambulances and screaming girls shouting, 'Leave it, he's not worth it!' were replaced by an altogether different beast. Oh, there were people sprawled over benches, doorways and floors, but a-huggin' and a-lovin' was the new a-punchin' and a-kickin'. Ecstasy had landed. In a big big way.

The Summer of Love had put paid to football violence! I knew the Ecstasy tablet was a love drug after moving in with a bird on the Haygate Estate. Not too much time for violence then.

After 1988, football hooliganism had already slightly changed. Millwall had got promoted to the First Division after our 103-year wait. Policing had increased in the top flight. It was easier to be a hooligan in the lower leagues. Then came the drug and Ecstasy revolution. For me, the next couple of years went by with relatively little trouble. Some of Millwall's biggest games passed by without any incident. During this period, it wasn't unusual to go to a rave or a club and see members of other London firms. On one night, we went to a warehouse rave in Clink Street, in a mad, labyrinthine building. (It was originally built as Britain's first prison, hence 'put in the clink'). So we were out in the club, about 15 of the Millwall boys, when a few West Ham faces known to us came in. There was some discussion between us about what to do. This was a completely alien situation for us. To be in a club with West Ham fans. Our natural instinct was to attack them, but this was a different situation. We were all off our heads on Es. We couldn't organise a round of drinks, let alone a charge into these West Ham fans. Luckily for us, they were in the same state. Don't get me wrong, we were hardly all best mates for the night, but a mutual, drug-driven unspoken peace pact was arrived at. That would never have happened on the piss. The exact opposite, in fact.

This was also the start of something else, something big. The drugs trade was a very lucrative business for the young entrepreneur. These tablets were being sold for £25. If bought in bulk, you could easily double your outlay money. Club nights began popping up all round London – Spectrum at Heaven, The Trip at the Astoria. These clubs were rammed with people. Not like an old, sweaty nightclub with 30 piss-head lads in it. These places were getting hundreds in every night.

Warehouse parties were popping up all over the place, too. If you sold 100 pills a week, that'd be a nice wage of £1,250 in the late Eighties. Still serious money today. With the illegal raves came the opportunity to make even more money. One day, we heard from a DJ friend of ours that he was going to do a rave in a field just outside the M25. The actual location was to be kept a secret. There was a telephone number that you had to phone at the last minute. We got ready by getting hold of some empty capsules off my mate's bird, who worked in a chemist. Plus a couple of ounces of speed and some trips. We made up our own capsules – and added half a trip. Come the night, we had 200 capsules done up.

The location was near Sevenoaks in Kent, in the middle of a field with a massive sound system and lasers. There were three of us. I stayed in the car with the drugs while the other two split up and sold the capsules. We had them bagged up into 25 caps a bag. When you had done your bag, you would go back to the car and drop the money back. That way you weren't walking about with loads of money. It was a funny sight. Me in the car with a Rambo knife in one hand and a can of CS gas next to the other. Two bags between my feet, one with capsules, one with money. We cleaned up – £25 a go. We made more in one night in a field than we could all week in the clubs.

We had a right blast for a couple of years, all loved up, although a few took the dreaded one-way ticket on the trip-train out of town. I heard about one kid that was selling acid. I have a funny feeling he was a novice because he stashed about 50 inside his sock before entering a club. Nobody asked him for one until about 20 minutes of him dancing away in a hot, sticky, packed rave. He went to the toilet to get them out but they had all disappeared. Dissolved into his skin. Ten minutes later, he was stretchered out to an ambulance. He never came back to planet earth again. Drugs, like hooliganism, can be a dangerous sport.

We had a few little skirmishes during this time but nothing major – except for when Hibs came to town and tried to take liberties in the late summer of 1990. We were still going to the games but half the time we had tablets still in us.

Football had a rebirth in the Nineties, with Sky and the new Premier League. Tons of money and live footie on the box. Everyone thinks that is what restarted the turnstiles clicking, Sky and the new Premier League. Bullshit! We stopped importing Ecstasy. Little back-street kitchens started knocking up their own, the tablets went down the pan and we needed a new kick again. So we went back to football. And fighting. Simple! Well, that's my theory. And I'm fucking sticking to it.

Funny really. Millwall Football Club waited 103 years to get to the top flight and we spent half the time mashed off our tits on Ecstasy. Oh, to relive those glory days.

splitting us up and trying to grab people and nick them. A few of our boys got nicked and taken away. I was mashed but just about had my head together enough to realise it was time for me to get out of there. I was away with a big mass of others so was feeling safe. A couple of quick scans back showed me even more Old Bill had swarmed in and got the situation under control. Forest were herded off towards Surrey Quays station.

Me and the boys headed back to The Tropics. Fighting is quite a sobering experience. Head had been cleared by a bit of adrenalin. A few more pints topped the day and topped the weekend off. Plus we were still in with a good shout of promotion to the Premier League.

23

MARSHALLING
THE TROOPS

We are the Millwall Bushwackers. The name is adopted and adapted from groups known as Bushwackers that would ambush people and towns during the American Civil War. This name originated in the early Eighties, an era of prominent football hooliganism. The original firm associated with Millwall was known as F-Troop, which just fizzled out. Younger kids came through and us older boys joined forces with them. There was no particular day that the F-Troop became he Bushwackers – it just evolved. F-Troop was actually a TV series in the Sixties, about a gang of Southern soldiers. There are lots of the original F-Troop chaps in our firm today, old mates of Harry the Dog, who has evolved into a mythological figure like Keyser Söze.

We were probably the most active firm in the Eighties. Our primary purpose was to cause trouble and fights at every Millwall football match. We were blamed for causing some of the worst acts of rioting in British football. Obviously, the firm still exists today. Some might think it is not as large as it was at its height in those days. They would put this down in part to ex-Millwall chairman Theo Paphitis and the introduction of a membership scheme. This followed the events outside The New Den on the evening of the Birmingham City play-off semi-final in May 2002. One Sergeant Russell Lamb of the Metropolitan Police Service, apparently an old veteran of the May Day and Poll Tax riots, described this as the worst violence he had ever experienced. But West Ham in 2009 proved conclusively that Millwall can be as big as ever if the occasion arises.

I would estimate that we can still put a mob together of 2,000, all intent on damage. Not just numbers, but men prepared to go into battle. The reasons for our longevity at the top of the hooligan tree are multiple. The tradition and toughness of the area defines the people in it. That image of a hard-working, hard-drinking, hard-fighting, hard-man bred from a life on the docks has unquestionably been passed down the generations. It is virtually genetic now. Fighting and violence was the norm, a laugh even. A skill and art passed from father to son, uncle to nephew, brother to brother and mate to mate. The amount of people that boxed in my area was phenomenal; it felt like everyone had a go at boxing. Self-protection was paramount and you had to learn quick. Terrace traditions are quickly learnt, too, and fighting is tradition number one.

The importance of Millwall Football Club to the community was incalculable. We seldom have glory days – it could be that lack of glory that has spurred us on at fighting, too. You fuck us on the pitch and we will fuck you off it. Done deal. Our honours list could be written on a Post-it note and you'd still have enough space for 'Harry Roberts Is Our Friend'. An in-built dislike and distrust of the police has also acted as a bond for the firm; no one wants to go near them. Ever. We stick together.

After the 1977 documentary, a lot of the firm probably played it all up a bit. Harry the Dog was the most infamous. Some of us older boys reckon the press created this monster.

One major reason we are the top firm is because we have no leader. Nobody could stand up and say, 'I am the leader of the firm.' Nobody. This has been more beneficial than anything. Once Spartacus goes down, the troops all start to panic. Once the leader collapses, then all are in disarray. I have seen it with so many other firms down the years; their main man gets taken out of the equation and they shit blue lights. Never in all my years in going was that remotely close to happening with Millwall. Factions were the key.

Our little faction is about 40–50 strong when everyone is out. No leader. Top boys are recognised – and I am not blowing my own trumpet too loud to say I am probably perceived as one of the top boys in our firm – but I am no leader. Nobody is. There must be another couple of firms about our size. A fair few from each firm will interact, they will know and contact each other. What time you meeting? Where at? How you getting there? Fundamentals.

The mini-firms all range in size totalling thirties, twenties, tens, maybe a mini-mob of eight, five, two or just one geezer on his own. Put it all together and you have the most vicious, violent, brutal, hardest firm – all prepared to stand their ground and fight – that the UK, Europe and probably the world has ever had the misfortune to encounter. Like any firm, it has got its absolute head-cases – people who take it too far. Which is why there have been deaths at games, Millwall included. Fortunately, they are a tiny minority. 'A good piss-up, a good punch-up and a good game of football – that is what Millwall is all about.' Yes, for many years, I have loved playing my part in The Bushwackers.

Meeting points were typical for a home game – The Gregorian Arms, The Bramcote Arms, The Gardeners, The Tropics, The Ancient Foresters. No great arrangements were necessary. It has been going on for over 40 years and everyone can find their way blindfolded.

The organisation of away trips was always done a couple of ways. Usually, we would arrange meeting points for everyone to get together. Pubs, train stations or towns on the way. We may all have been on the same train in the early days, lots began to hire coaches once we realised we were going to get wrapped up by the Old Bill, or do the early bird run and give the police the slip that way. Now it is all done with texts, e-mails, phone calls and the Internet. In the early days, information was spread by word of mouth, always changing to keep the Old Bill on their toes. The grapevine at Millwall was a lively place to have your ears pinned.

Some of the firms we battled with included the 6.57 Crew, Aston Villa Hardcore, Baby Squad, Birmingham Zulus, The Casuals, Chelsea Headhunters, Derby Lunatic Fringe, Leeds United Service Crew, Luton Town MIGs, The Muckers, Soul Crew and Yid Army and, of course, our main rivals – West Ham's ICF. You've got to laugh at some of the names. Fucking pathetic.

The camaraderie, the spirit, togetherness, everyone watching each other's back … that feeling of belonging to something. The security of it all. There are 60-year-old men right down to 13-year-old boys. Why was there no major hooliganism during our two years in the top flight? Bigger clubs spend more on policing – simple as that. They didn't want the top flight of English football sullied by Millwall. Every game, we were surrounded by Old Bill. Every away game, we were boxed in at all sides. The second season, once we knew we were going down, we left our mark on a few places. But nothing major. Only a little 'Millwall was here'. In retrospect, it's much easier being a hooligan in the lower leagues. The clubs do not have the funds that the big boys do. We could and did get away with a lot more lower down the league pyramid.

Before 1977, Millwall hadn't done anything that any other football team's fans hadn't done – the dud hand grenade aside. Other than never getting turned over by any other firm, that is. The coffin on the pitch came later. The only difference was Millwall were picked for the *Panorama* documentary. After that, everything changed. All of a sudden, the fans changed.

In all other hooligan firms, they want to rise through the ranks and reach the top. And that is the sort of mentality of your average hooligan. How they would love to be the top man of their firm. Replace the top man. That is not the case at Millwall; we do not have a top man. So how can you want to be a person that does not exist? Nobody wants to be top man. There is no pyramid like in all the other firms. We are more like a cylinder or a cube that is solid right the way through. If football didn't exist, if the national sport was tiddlywinks, Millwall would be the number-one firm of tiddlywink hooligans.

24

WELSH LAMBS TO THE SLAUGHTER

First game of the 1999/2000 season. No better way to start it off than with a trip to the land were men are men and sheep are scared. Wales. Cardiff City. We all met at Paddington Station. It was a red-hot day and it was all shorts and summer tans, fresh from the break over the summer holidays. Eleven of us had just enjoyed two weeks of peace and quiet in Zante, half-a-dozen Millwall boys and five from work; it was their holiday and we just hijacked it. Ready now to get back to business. There was no time to go on the rip in London so we sorted a few crates between us for the trip – Stella (AKA 'wife-beater', although on a day like today, AKA 'Welsh-beater').

The first train left with about 30 of the chaps on it, the rest were following on the next train, a further 250 on the old football special. They don't want football fans mingling with the public. I missed the first train and got the second 20 minutes later. As for the first train cargo, 30 top boys, brave boys, knowing back-up was the other side of the Severn. What was in their heads? Numbers and safety don't enter your head at that stage.

It is not something that will faze you. It just doesn't – we revert to instincts. They take over. Fight or flight. Fuck the danger! When the first train pulled into Cardiff station, everything seemed quiet, the 30 exited the station. The silence was broken.

'Soul Crew ... Soul Crew ...'

There were about 200 Taffies waiting. Without hesitation, the Millwall 30 ran at Cardiff; they clashed head-on. This tactic shocked them and, after the first exchange, Cardiff turned and ran.

A couple of the boys were telling me, as I well know, it was not a case of throwing combinations and jabs in that situation or any other situation like that. It's fucking big haymakers and concentrating on making them count. No weapons were carried by our 30. They were straight off the train and straight into The Soul Crew. After they turned tail, our boys took over a pub in Cardiff town centre. The second train arrived with the other 250 of us. We all met up in the pub and were waiting for another attack. It didn't take long.

They started throwing things at the pub – bottles, bricks, coins, lighters and anything they could get their hands on. No one was injured. Not one. The Soul Crew are not very good at throwing things, it seems. No damage to the pub either. We were all stood outside this boozer that was in a row of shops with just a few tables and chairs on the pavement. There was no damage to it whatsoever. They were safely keeping their distance. We charged them. They ran away. We stood outside and couldn't believe how easy it had been so far. Then came another attack. A repeat performance – missile-throwing from a distance. We charged and they ran. After the second attack, we were surrounded by the Old Bill, who kept us in the pub.

They didn't want any trouble from Millwall; they let us carry on drinking. A few police were around but not enough to stop us when we charged. It was one of those instances where the few

Old Bill around were not going to endanger themselves to stop two firms from having a fight. There are times when the Old Bill – even with plenty of them there and plenty of back-up – just stand back and let you crack on. Like Spurs in 2001, when about 100 of us attacked 100 Spurs, about 30 Old Bill just stood back and watched as both firms had a right go at each other.

By the time of the escort, about 1,200–1,500 Millwall were there for the game. The police had put a ring around us. Outside that was another ring of Old Bill. Outside them were the dogs. We were totally surrounded by riot police – helmets with their numbers on the back; black boiler suits; leg pads; gloves; truncheons. I think it's meant to intimidate as much as protect, all the gear they wear. They look like fucking clowns to me.

A couple of big riot vans in the front were leading the way. A couple of the big meat wagons came behind, each one full to the brim with more back-up. They obviously needed it; we are evil. With 30 on the first train and 250 on the second, plus a few late stragglers that couldn't get out of bed that morning, it totted up to about 300 of The Bushwackers – the most violent, vicious fuckers of all the hooligan firms they encounter each season. (F-troop, our predecessors, were probably the first ones to have a name). I call us 'The Bushwackers', but we never actually said the name. No one in our firm ever uttered the words 'The Bushwackers'. I know the name is used regularly when people talk about Millwall's firm, yet inside the firm, it is rarely uttered. The fact was, we were 300 of Millwall's top, top boys in Cardiff.

On the way to the ground, Cardiff tried to get to us from the side through a park. A fair few hundred of them were sort of trying to get at us anyway. They had probably broken through some sort of police cordon or police lines, so maybe I do the Soul Crew a disservice there. But I doubt it. I know we were fucking mad to get to them. The Old Bill had truncheons drawn and plenty of big Alsatians. Get past the first one and the second one pushed you back. Get past the second one and Welsh Lassie, a rabid, foaming lump of a dog who hadn't been fed for three days because Millwall were coming, was their third line of defence. The first line was strong; they pushed you back with one hand and had their 2ft truncheons lifted over their heads at the ready, or the spring cosh, or T-bar truncheons and batons at the ready. The *Heddlu* were working hard to keep us in check.

My mind was totally taken off attacking them by the police helicopter, one of the funniest things I have ever seen at a football game. The Soul Crew were in the park and had a big fence to get over, but they didn't get near that. We were still being shunted along towards the ground by the professional crowd control experts at a fairly rapid pace. But that helicopter! I couldn't take my eyes off it. They were obviously keeping Cardiff back somewhere. But I was still watching this helicopter, thinking, 'Is he going to land that fucking thing in the park? He can't land that fucking thing in the park ... he's landed that fucking thing in the park!'

It worked – for the police. Cardiff Soul Crew scattered. Think ten-pin bowling then times it by fifty. Fucking funny watching all The Soul Crew skittled by the chopper. The escort must have lasted about 20–30 minutes. No one broke in and no one broke out.

We got to the ground and the match went on with the usual back and forth verbals, Cardiff screaming all the anti-English songs they love so much: 'Fuck the Queen', 'Argentina ... Argentina ... Argentina ... Argentina ...', 'Always shit on the English side of the bridge ...' (to the tune of 'Always Look on the Bright Side of Life'). Tickles me, that one.

'Argentina' is a favourite of theirs. Maradona's Hand of God from the 1986 World Cup, and the World Cup in 1998 after

Beckham's petulant little flick, all still fresh in their minds. We are Londoners. We are Millwall. We are English. We are in a foreign country. And so we all understand their chants. They see us as English first and foremost, see. Funny like! No doubt, some of their Soul Crew have been nicked at England games; and stupid, too, seeing that some Welsh guards had also died at the Falkland Islands. We retorted with 'No Surrender' and our Welsh favourite, 'Sheep ... sheep ... sheep ... shaggers!'

At the end of the match, we were locked in by the Old Bill. At the time, the away end was uncovered so we were sitting ducks. It seemed like anything that was not bolted down was raining down on us. We tried to kick the side doors open but the Old Bill were holding them shut. We decided to get out another way. 'Pitch!'

There is no conference in these situations. Some heavy-duty shit is raining down on you. There is no 'OK, chaps, what do we all think about the virtues of removing ourselves from this raining debris? Now let us see a show of hands – ayes to the left, nays to the right ... ayes just about take it!' Fuck off!

The pitch. One voice shouted it. One went. He was up and over and we all went. That is the Millwall way. We piled on to the pitch and ran towards the main stand, down the stairs and underneath the stadium. We kicked the doors off the grandstand to get at them. I happened to be right at the front. Three of us were kicking fuck at the door. It finally burst open. As it swung open, I remember a mop came flying over my right shoulder. A fucking mop! Who said Millwall don't fight clean? When we opened the doors we were met by a sea of Soul Crew. Straight out into the car park we steamed. I hit the nearest Taffy to me. My favourite right haymaker, bang on the top of his head. He fell sideways to the floor. They weren't expecting this complete surprise attack. There was me, a young kid and a fella about my age. I knew their faces but they were from the different firms that all come together to make one big firm on match day. One of the other two, I didn't see which, threw a dig and put another on his arse. It was then time to retreat. Three against the sea? Not good odds. Suicide. You ain't got a fucking chance. We are evil; we are not stupid. So having put a few on their arses, we then retreated into the concourse under the stand. This was to our advantage, because as they came through the doors they were getting picked off one by one.

One came at me. The right did the damage once again. As he was falling, he grabbed my shirt. Someone kicked his legs and he hit the deck. I booted him clean in the face. Then booted him clean in the face again. It did some damage. Some of us were getting hit, too. But concentrate. Concentrate. Hit! Don't get hit! Hit! Don't get hit! Then we were getting pushed back.

I was stepping over Welsh bodies. Must have been about three or four Soul Crew on the floor as I stepped backwards, treading all over them. They were just helpless on the floor. A few more boots went flying in as we were going backwards. They just kept coming and managed to push us back by sheer weight of numbers – with the individual fighting we were still on top. The Old Bill came storming in and got between us. We regrouped on the pitch ready for another go but they had it under control now.

We were not exactly unscathed ourselves. One lad of ours had a bad cut over his eye. He was covered in claret all down his face and all down his shirt. He wasn't dazed or nothing like that. Cuts look a lot worse than they actually are. A couple of stitches would have seen him right and he would be back for the next game.

On the pitch, we got surrounded again. Herded like animals – but we are not. The fighting – the hooliganism – it is sport for us. This is consenting adults. It is like-minded people doing something they get pleasure out of. I can totally understand why people are appalled and sickened; my dad always was. But try to understand in return the pleasure that we get out of it! No? Never mind. We are all different and that will suffice.

They put us back in the away end. All the Cardiff were out of the ground now. No more shite raining down on us. They kept us there for another 15 minutes or so. No Cardiff boys had stuck around while we were being detained. There was a swift frog-march down to the station and we were off back to Paddington on a dry run. Alcohol free. Then meeting up with the boys from my firm. Answering questions ... asking questions ... a bit of a debriefing and having a laugh. Only with our firm members and in quiet conversation. Even faces that you know – you do not talk with them about it, what you have done or what they have done. You never know who is on that train. You question everything and you are cautious about everyone. That is the mentality of a hooligan, especially of a Millwall hooligan. You are only one stupid boast from being arrested.

So the walk back to the station was uneventful. If The Soul Crew had really wanted to make a fist of it on this day, why did they not stick around for another 20 minutes or so? My guess is they took the opportunity to get the fuck out of there. And who said the Welsh are stupid? Looking back on it, Cardiff were game, but let themselves down a bit by running away throughout the day.

From what I have heard, Cardiff books portray a totally different story about this particular day. Never! Shocking, eh? Well, Cardiff are bound to do that, aren't they? It is clearly done to enhance their reputation. After all, there is only one way to become the king of the jungle and that is to beat the lion. And if you cannot beat the king of the jungle, then just lie about it.

All this from little Welsh rarebits who were ripped apart at Brighton. Twice. A fact I am led to believe is omitted from the same book. Never let the truth get in the way of a good story, they say. It would appear The Soul Crew live and write by that belief because apparently they attacked the pub we were in. Ripped us apart. Turned us over. Chased us up the street. Hmm! The Lions must have been having a fucking big collective cat nap, because not one of us saw any of that. Maybe it's because it just did not happen. If that is what they have written, then that is not the truth. We know what happened that day and we went home happy. It was the Lions v the Bluebirds. The Bluebirds were throwing things – gotta give them that. They threw a lot of things. Not particularly good throwers. Think it's because of their wings, myself. Oh, and they can definitely take flight. So credit where credit is due there.

We were given the freedom of Wales – their pubs, their stadium, their town. The Lions roared and the Bluebirds chirruped in response. The biggest problem for us was catching that irritating, chirpy little shit of a Bluebird! Which just about sums up that day. We were there for a good ruck and they really did not want to know after a couple of exchanges where they came off much worse. And that *is* the truth.

When we had them at home that season, they did not bring a big firm. There were reports that 100 more were intercepted on the way to The Den. It was a poor show against a team that has come to your town and took the piss all day. After that season, all our matches were changed to midweek or had restrictions. Then came the 2004 Cup Final at the Millennium Stadium in Cardiff; a perfect opportunity for The Soul Crew to get revenge. Nothing. Not a thing. We were looking for them everywhere. Not very good from the self-proclaimed kings of Wales. Kings of Wales! Oh, very good, yes!

Well done the Soul-Less, Soldier-Less Crew. They always remind me of the song – 'All These Things That I've Done'. It goes, *'I've got soul, but I'm not a soldier ... I've got soul, but I'm not a soldier'.* Ironically, it's by The Killers.

Four months after we had been running about in Cardiff, it was the Taffies' turn to come to The Den. After what we had done in their city, we thought they would be bringing a top firm to London. We had a good little firm in The Bramcote Arms, about 100, all ages.

News came through from London Bridge that Cardiff were on their way to South Bermondsey train station. We flew out of the pub and headed for the station. A lot of people took their bottles and pints with them so they could finish their drinks and have a makeshift weapon after. These cunts were going to get a reception! We were expecting a firm hell-bent on having a go on our manor. The short march was about 100 yards.

We got to the station entrance on Ilderton Road. The Old Bill were camped outside but we knew a charge from two game firms either side of them would cause some gaps, allowing us to get at each other. Millwall were starting to mob up. We had about 400 outside the station. People were giving verbal to the Old Bill, who were getting twitchy. They knew the Cardiff fans were due any minute.

The train pulled in on the platform above. There was a surge to break police lines to enter the station but the Old Bill stood firm. From the top of the stairs came The Soul Crew. As they reached the bottom, we attacked the police line in front of the station trying to get at them. Once again the line held. With all the police attention on us, this was a perfect opportunity for Cardiff to come at us. They stood behind the Old Bill ... waving! Waving their fucking arms. A poor effort from the Welsh.

The Old Bill brought in reinforcements and pushed us back to the corner of Ilderton Road and Rotherhithe New Road. A stand-off developed between Millwall and the police and about 20 of us moved on to the Bonamy estate and made our way to the ground. We went round to the East Stand Upper for the match which we won 3–0. The Taffies were safely tucked away in the North Stand Upper tier nowhere near us. So they began to get braver with more arm-waving and anti-English songs.

After the match, we made our way to The Bramcote to group up and have a go. Another group had started to congregate by The Golden Lion. We waited until the escort was on Ilderton Road and attacked. The police line held firm once again. Cardiff were not interested in a tear-up. They were more than happy behind the safety of the police. We were now fighting with the Old Bill. A running battle had started with them chasing us back with baton charges and us running them back with fireworks, bottles, bricks and anything we could get our hands on. We were still determined to get at Cardiff. More reinforcements arrived and they pushed us back to Rotherhithe New Road again. Then one Old Bill decided to drive a police van past us outside The Golden Lion. He got caught behind a car and had to slow down. He was pelted with bottles and bricks and the windows were put through as the coppers cowered inside. They made a decision to get out of there. He mounted the pavement and drove down it with all his windows smashed.

With Cardiff on the train, we made our way to The Ancient Foresters for a drink. The young kids carried on the pelting of the Old Bill and smashing things up. This went on well into the night. We had a good piss-up to the background noise of police sirens.

25

THE LIONS LEAVE
THE DEN

Our most famous ground was The Den in New Cross, SE14, which we moved to in 1910. We had previously occupied no fewer than four separate grounds on the Isle of Dogs in the 25 years since our formation as a football club. Tom Thorne, the director in charge, had sought the help of architect Archibald Leitch and builders Humphries of Knightsbridge to build The Den, and the estimated cost was £10,000.

The first match to be played there was against Brighton & Hove Albion, who spoiled the celebrations by winning 0–1. Before kick-off, a brass lion, inscribed (in Gaelic) 'We Will Never Turn Our Backs To The Enemy' was presented to the club. The Millwall Roar was born, with The Den becoming one of the most feared grounds in the country. No team liked to play there, because the crowd and the place itself created such an intimidating atmosphere.

Many supporters from the East End of London continued to follow The Lions in the early years. After our move south of the River Thames, supporters would walk through the Greenwich foot tunnel to join the new fans drawn mainly from the Surrey Docks. The Lions' fans were tough, uncompromising and quick to speak their minds and offer advice to the team and officials. Anyone visiting The Den thinking that Southerners were soft soon realised they were in the wrong part of London.

On 8 May 1993, Bristol Rovers came to The Den for its last ever game. What a day! We all started early. A full English in a café to sort myself out from the night before. Then we all met up at The Duke of Windsor down the Old Kent Road. 11.00am – not knocking on the door, but not long after. A bit of planning had gone into this day and so all our firm were there pretty early.

Now I'm not saying we were looking forward to it – this strange, new ground, the fear of the unknown, leaving The Den, which had been our home for 83 years. It had been a fortress for us; teams were intimidated. I was also aware that this new stadium had a capacity of 20,000-plus, at a time when our average attendance was around 10,000. The ground had been built with four separate sides ready for the next step up – the Premier League. I wanted to believe in that plan. But if any Millwall fan was being truly honest with themselves, well ... not too many really did believe.

It was a different atmosphere in the pub from the usual home game. Something a bit special was happening that day. There were about 20 of us in there. People coming and going all day. I was propping the bar up for most of that time. Had about ten pints, plus a few chasers – brandy, or neat scotch. Lots of conversation going on all over. Some people wanting the move and some not. A busy few hours. What time are you going? What do you reckon about this move? Where are you going in the ground?

We stayed in The Duke of Windsor right up to the kick-off. The boozer was rammed by noon. Everyone, and I mean everyone, was milling around. All the old faces, people I hadn't seen for ages. All the floaters. The mood? There was a funny atmosphere. Some were in party spirits, but there was a hint of sadness in the air, too.

By one o'clock, I'd had a right skinful. We were just having a laugh. Topping up from the night before. Most of our firm were lagging by this time. Still two hours until kick-off. We were chatting – the usual shite: what we all got up to last night; who got laid with who and where; what she did and what she wouldn't do. No one mentioned for ages the fact that this was our last ever game at The Den.

At 2.30pm we started heading to the ground. Bristol Rovers fans were dotted around. They were safe. Although no one said anything – no one stood on a table and said, 'No trouble today, chaps!'

It just wasn't on the agenda; everyone knew that. People were just not in that mood. We weren't interested in the away fans. This was the last day at The Den. As we approached the stadium, the mood was a bit of a mixed bag. Some people were laughing and joking, and others ... well, sadness was etched on more than a few faces. A few of the Millwall boys were having a chat and a bit of banter with some of the Bristol Rovers boys. It was that kind of day. Big crowd, way bigger than normal. It was going to be a full house.

I was making my way up Cold Blow Lane towards the turnstiles. There was a real sombre mood in the queue. It hit home then. This is our last ever game at the old ground. Memories were racing through my head as it was my turn to click in. 1984, Swansea – Bill Roffey's 30-yard screamer; 1987, Sheringham's goal against Stoke – 2–0; we won at Hull the next game and secured promotion to the top flight.

My last ever entrance fee was paid. Can't even remember how much it was to get in but I paid my dues and walked up to the halfway line straight on to the terraces. The atmosphere in the ground was totally different. Looking around and soaking it all up. This had been our home for 83 years. A roller-coaster of emotions. Taking it all in. Feeling sad but looking forward to the promise of top-flight football. A whole new chapter starting in a new stadium. I wasn't there thinking, 'This is the worst day of my life.'

On the one hand, we were sad to see the old place go; on the other, we were moving on to bigger and better things. People are creatures of habit. Most of the older boys probably wanted to stay. Us younger ones wanted to be part of the new football revolution – Sky Television, a whole new era. I wanted to be a part of it. All this money being thrown at the game. I wanted to believe the hype. This move was going to enable us to get to the Premier League.

The Den was totally fucked at this stage and completely run down, with terrible facilities. Two or three toilets where we stood and fellas just pissed on the floor at the big games. But it was all we knew. There was no standing on ceremony at The Den. A load of booze down your neck and there was a party atmosphere – and what a party atmosphere there was that day.

The first thing I noticed was some fella on the roof of one of the stands dressed as a lion. On the roof … as a lion! The mood was set. We were going to have fun. Everyone in the ground, I felt, was up for it. The game kicked off. It was weird; no one was interested in the game. It was a nothing game anyway. I'm sure that the first time the ball was kicked into the terraces, it was swallowed up by the crowd. The first ball out of touch never came back. I think that happened every time the ball was kicked into the stands. Oh, we were all after souvenirs. How many balls Millwall went through that day I don't know, but I'm sure we ran out. I was lagging but there was a definite delay while they went and got some more balls. About ten people walked away with a match ball that day, it must have been. Probably more.

The first pitch invasion happened after about 20 minutes. One geezer jumped on and a few others joined him. The sell-out crowd were all laughing; this wasn't an invasion by The Bushwackers. However, after about the fourth invasion, they were getting shouted off the pitch by the crowd. We got beat 3–0 or 4–0; it didn't matter. No one cared. Everyone was getting ready to get their souvenir. One fella couldn't wait. He ran on with about five minutes to go and grabbed a shirt off one of the players. As soon as the final whistle went, the race was on.

I was away … on to the pitch … to the goal. Then into the Cold Blow Lane Stand. Grabbed my piece of turf … grabbed my bit of the net … ripped one of the seats out. Job done. With my three souvenirs sorted, I looked out over the pitch. The whole playing surface was covered in a sea of people. Three or four of the players were down to their pants – shirts, shorts, boots gone. They were all fair game this day. The players played along. So did the Old Bill. They stood back and let everyone do what they wanted to do. They were not going to get too involved on a day like today. I looked around the ground and noticed one old boy with tears in his eyes.

I had my souvenirs and went straight home. Some day it had been. Drained. Totally emotionally drained after the match. I put my piece of turf in my little window box. The net was placed on the wall. I didn't know what to do with the seat so I shoved it on the top of my cupboard. It stayed there for years. The turf was watered religiously every morning and every night as if my life depended on it. It died ten days later!

The new season would be at The New Den.

26

NAUGHTY ... AND
NOT VERY NICE

The Naughty Forty, Stoke City's firm, have always seemed to give us a hostile reception at their place. Never truly threatening us, more of a verbal threat than a physical show. Nor have they ever really done much at Millwall. Not too many have. There was the pointless incident in the mid-Nineties when they smashed up The Tropics at 9.00am, one of our main pubs on the corner of Rotherhithe New Road and Galloway Road. When it was shut. With no one in it. Which was a bit ... well ... pointless. Another one of the pubs that has gone from the Millwall area.

On 21 October 2000, about 200 of us met up at London Bridge. A couple of our firm were missing on this day – work commitments, money worries, 'er indoors, kids' Christmas presents ... us hooligans have these issues, too, you know. We piled onto the Tube at London Bridge. The Japanese tourists were freaked out by us. The girls who stray into one of these carriages – although totally safe – are always deemed fair game. It's never the time nor the place, but it never seems to stop one or two of the boys from having a go. You've got to remember, Mr Testosterone is rampant at this stage, mingling and adding to Mr Adrenalin, Mr Alcohol and Mr Cocaine. Not too many suits are on the Tubes on a Saturday, but the tourists are always freaked out. Most people are struck static. They are in no danger from us but I have seen some petrified people on these journeys. Understandable really. Understandable, too, that they try to avoid eye contact and you can see them thinking, 'Please ... please, go away ... please, make yours the next stop ... please, don't look at me.'

On this day, 200 of us, many dressed alike with baseball caps, jeans, similar jackets and trainers, have all piled on to the Tube to get from London Bridge to Euston. As ever, the passengers on the train visibly stiffen. One second they are having a quiet, peaceful little ride under the River Thames and the next is slightly different. Members of the most notorious hardcore hooligan firm in the Western world have boarded their carriage. On the way to a fight. It is quite a scene.

The beers were flowing on the train. We only take enough beer for the journey there and have got this down to a T. We know how many cans we are going to drink on the way and it is no good having crates of beer left over because it will all be taken off you. When we got to Stoke, we were drinking our last tin of Stella. I knew everyone was hyped up for an afternoon of fun.

When we arrived, there was a heavy police presence. That was the usual stuff for us at this stage. We are Millwall; we are evil. Dogs and meat wagons all around the station. Riot police in all their gear. It is a bit of a cat-and-mouse game with the Old Bill. I was thinking if we get there late this day, we can swerve the police escort and say hello to the Naughty Forties. Sometimes, we will get off a stop or two before our scheduled station and make our own way there. It is all about trying to stay out of that police escort. Steer clear of that and fun and games could be in store. When that big, horrible, black cat wraps its paws around you it is very difficult and sometimes completely impossible to escape its grasp. It is a big part of an away trip. Their objectives? Well, it's not hard to picture the scene at police HQ. All the Old Bill in a big hall the morning of the match. The Chief Super flicks on his overhead projector and lights up the board. Slides his transparent sheet under the lamp and flashes up his bullet points:

- Get the Millwall fans under control
- Get them into the ground
- Get them back on their train
- Get them the fuck out of our city

The police know how to play this game in some cities and have not got a clue in others. Whenever we have travelled up to Merseyside to play Everton, the Old Bill has wrapped us up there. Whereas in the Midlands – clueless. Whenever we have gone up to Coventry, Wolves, Birmingham and Leicester, totally fucking clueless. The Met Police do this shit every week. With all the London clubs, they have a massive operation and have maybe five or six games every Saturday on average. They have got to police inside and outside the stadiums before, during and after the game – Tube stations, railways, pubs. A lot of policing but a lot of opportunities to escape their claws. We can jump off early and go for a few drinks in a pub but, once they hear about us, they surround that pub. You are fucked. The lions can't roar. They tell us what time we are leaving the pub. None of that 'We'll have two more here and pop along to the next one.' Forget it. They send someone to the front of the pub. 'You'll be off in ten minutes,' or 'You'll be here for another hour.' A lot of the time, someone will ask them what is happening. 'What's going on here? Are we staying or getting moved on or what?'

The authorities obviously see the problem as one of crowd control. Measures have been increasingly strengthened – more police, more horses, more dogs, closer surveillance, CCTV, being herded like animals, cages and spikes introduced, fans firmly separated, body searches – all this combined with a broader definition of hooliganism, has resulted in everybody feeling a hardening of police attitudes towards football fans. Never mind just us hooligans. Once, going to Man City, we managed to completely fool them. We got off at Stockport. A good number of us ended up in a little pub at the station – early, too, about 12.30pm. Someone had a contact at Manchester United. They came up, got annihilated and ran away.

On this day, we were escorted straight to the ground. We got in just before kick-off and the Stoke fans were giving it from the start. Although we were separated by netting over the seats and lines of stewards, we made a charge at the Stoke fans. Clean over the netting and through the stewards. Twenty at the front tried to stand their ground but took a beating. A couple of one-on-ones. One Millwall threw a punch and their fella went back as it cracked him on the jaw. A couple more of theirs tried to have a little go, but the Naughty Forties were not being so naughty. They really did not want to know. Backing off and backing off until the reinforcements arrived in the form of the Old Bill. The riot cops moved in looking to nick any one in their way. Us 20 pile back over the netting. No one got nicked and we all faded back into the crowd.

In the second half, Stoke seemed to become a lot braver behind the line of police dressed in riot gear, who were only interested in looking our way. Just before the end of the game, Stoke scored. This caused them to start giving it and jumping around, so we tried to shut them up with chairs, coins, lighters and anything we could get our hands on.

We made a quick exit out of the ground to get at them. Some of the Stoke fans had set themselves up behind a metal chain-link fence. We were getting hit by bricks, bottles, lumps of wood, even pierced cans of CS gas. They soon came unstuck after the Old Bill steamed into the Stoke firm to try and disperse them. This sent them from behind the safety of the fence into the car park. Heaven! With all the Old Bill concentrated behind the metal fence, it was a free-for-all.

I ran at one of them and threw a big right. It landed on the side of his head. That was enough for him. He staggered a bit, turned around and stumbled away as quickly as his wobbly legs allowed him. A little surge went on and we had hold of a couple of them. One was down on the floor and he was taking a few good punches to the head. He was not out for the count but if he had been asked the time or date, no way could that boy have given the correct answer. His eyes were bouncing all over. Another was rolled into a ball on the floor and he was taking a right good kicking. He had been trying to fight back but now he was in self-preservation mode, curled up like a little hedgehog. As people were running past he would take another kick. His head was down and he wished he was invisible. He was not. At least five full-blooded boots to the body he took as he was curled up. The Old Bill saved him from a worse beating as they tried to restore order. The Naughties had soon had enough and got on their toes followed by the Old Bill.

We were all rounded up and escorted to the station. A fair old walk, but the Naughty Forties had all gone home to lick their wounds. A couple of hours later we were back in The Ancient Foresters in Bermondsey. About 15 of us had a late one in London Bridge at St Christopher's. A good day out. We gave Stoke a proper hiding.

27

KICKING OFF AT THE NEW DEN

The opening of the new stadium – 4 August 1993 – and the first thing we all noticed was that there was no paying on the turnstile. It was a friendly against Sporting Lisbon, all-ticket and a sell-out. We got tickets for the West Upper. Can't remember why. The names of all the stands? West Upper, West Lower, East Upper, East Lower, South Upper, South Lower, North Upper, North Lower. You're having a laugh! £16 million spent on the first new stadium in London since the war, not one penny of that spent on any company or person to come up with names for the stands. North, South, East and West. Upper and lower. Fucking genius. The North Stand was designated the away end.

So The New Den becomes the new home of Millwall FC. It was originally called The New London Stadium. Not one Millwall supporter has ever referred to it as anything other than The Den. It is situated in Bermondsey, south-east London, almost directly adjacent to the railway line between London Bridge and New Cross Gate, near a big massive incinerator! It is about 300m from the original Den and it's built on the site of an old church at Senegal Fields.

Originally, it was planned to have a seating capacity of 25,000–30,000. However, we couldn't afford it. Instead, it has an all-seater capacity of 20,146. The average attendance for the 1993/94 season was just over 9,000. In 2000/01, it was 11,442. In 2005/06, it had declined to just 9,529. The 2008/09 season was 8,940. The average overall for 2009/10 was under 1,000. So it was probably a wise move not building a 30,000-seat arena. The players and fans would have been rattling round even more. The local press and fans' groups argued this was down to the membership scheme. People were being put off becoming members because of the intrusive nature of the information required before you were allowed to join. Two photos, two forms of ID, driving licence, passport and two utility bills – and you were charged for the privilege. The club raised £100,000. It was introduced by former club chairman Theo Paphitis after the Birmingham City game in 2002. Chief sportswriter of the *South London Press*, Toby Porter, put it best when he stated that the scheme '… whilst deterring the hooligan element also deterred decent, law-abiding fans who were reluctant to hand over sensitive personal information in order to watch a game of football'. In all honesty, it does not deter any firm's member. If you want a ticket for the match, you get a ticket for the match. So it is bought using someone else's name! Not going to lose sleep over that.

Our stadium was the first new, all-seater stadium to be completed after the Taylor report on the Hillsborough disaster. It was designed with effective crowd management in mind, given our history, notoriety and the crowd problems at the old Den. The escape routes were meant to be short and direct. And yet it took ten years for them to come up with a way of getting visiting fans out of there without us getting at them. The late Labour leader John Smith opened the stadium. The New Den became the sixth ground that we had occupied since our formation on the Isle of Dogs in 1885. Sixth! Don't think too many professional clubs have been involved in that many ground moves.

The Old Den was never used for anything. The New Den? Jesus! The cameras had never been at The Den so much. We should have seen Theo's move into the TV world coming. The New Den doubled as the Dragons' Lair, home ground of Harchester United in the TV series *Dream Team*. It also appeared in an episode of the ITV show *Primeval*. I wasn't there, but I didn't hear of any trouble. We even hosted the FA Cup Final. Oh yes. On 1 May 2006, the Women's FA Cup Final between Arsenal and Leeds was played there. Arsenal ladies apparently won the cup 5–0. I never went. There was no trouble.

It was also used to film an episode of *The Bill* during the home game against Leyton Orient in March 2008. There was no trouble. So they aired it in June 2008. On top of that, sportswear giant Nike filmed their 'Take it to the next level' advertisement over a period of three days and nights at The Den, also in March 2008. The firm weren't there. There was no trouble.

Honestly, this stuff has got to stop. Surely. No? Clearly Theo's influence rages on. We hosted the Samaritans' celebrity soccer sixes in May 2008, when film and television stars played at The Den, the first time the event had not been hosted by a Premier League club. Babyshambles failed to retain the trophy, losing 3–2 to dance act Faithless. The firm never went. There was no trouble. The winners of the women's trophy were Cansei de Ser Sexy. Around 150 celebrities took part including one old favourite of mine, Terry Hurlock. Also taking part were Amy Winehouse, McFly (not an old favourite of mine; we should have gone ... there would have been trouble), and Tony Hadley.

Fair play, they raised money for charity.

Mick McCarthy guided us to third place in the new Division One at the end of the 1993/94 season. We also knocked Arsenal out of the FA Cup in the third round by beating them 2–0, with a spectacular goal coming from young Irish midfielder Mark Kennedy, but we lost to Derby County in the play-off semifinals. McCarthy resigned to take charge of the Republic of Ireland national team in December 1995, shortly after we had been knocked off the top of the Division One table by Sunderland after a 6–0 defeat. Mark Kennedy was sold to Liverpool in March 1994 for £2,300,000. All the early dreams and claims from the boardroom had been shattered. Over £6,000,000 raised in transfer fees and no one to replace them. We were going mental.

Jimmy Nicholl of Raith Rovers was appointed as McCarthy's replacement. What a load of bollocks he was. We finished bottom after leading at Christmas. In five months, we had gone from the top of Division One, pushing for a place in the Premiership, to Division Two for the 1996/97 season. We also experienced 'extreme financial difficulties' that resulted in us being placed in administration for a short period of time. Jimmy Nicholl was 'relieved of his duties'. So at least something good came out of it. John Docherty returned on a short-term basis to stabilise the club at player level. It was clear the new ground move wasn't going to mean progression.

28

THE FIRM EARNS
ITS SPURS

We knew Spurs were bringing a firm when we played them in August 2001; they wanted to test themselves against a real firm. Obviously, arrangements were made and the old grapevine worked its usual magic. It had been a late one the night before so I rolled out of bed and took a quick yomp up to the pub. We met up early at The Gregorian on Jamaica Road. No food but plenty of boozing and cocaine, though. We had been in there for an hour and there were now about 100 of us. Spurs would be coming out of Bermondsey station and we were ready and waiting outside the pub. It's hardly a beer garden but it has got a couple of benches and about 15 of us were there. We all knew each other. You haven't got every person's mobile number but you know everyone and everyone knows you. You still talk mostly to those in your firm. The odd nod here and there to some … nothing at all to others. But we all know when it kicks off that we will all be sticking together. This meet was all pre-arranged. One of our boys was in contact with one of theirs.

There were a few coppers around but not many. The British Transport Police would have informed the Old Bill that 100 chaps wearing baseball caps and casual clothes had just boarded the train in north London heading to south-east London. The secret would be out by now.

We spotted them walking down either side of Jamaica Road. There are about ten in front of me and everyone else that exited the front of the pub was behind me. Front line. We attacked them from the side and trapped a mob of them against a railing in the middle of the road. I hit this fella with a peach of a right hook. Caught him flush on the temple. He fell back and ended up half on the floor and half against the railings. I booted him in the chest. He was covering up, dazed from the punch and winded from the kick. I booted him again. And again. Big grunts from him as they landed on his torso. All he knew at that stage was to keep covered as much as possible. The rest scattered. The ones taking a beating were rescued by the Old Bill turning up. No one wanted to get nicked. Straight back into the pub we all ran. All told, from spotting them to running back into the pub, it probably lasted about a minute.

The police weren't going to come into The Gregorian and start making arrests. They would be more concerned with getting Spurs out of there before it went off again. We carried on drinking until it was time to make our way to the ground for the match. I had probably swallowed ten pints during that session.

All through the game Spurs were giving it the usual bravado – loads of arm-waving and the usual sing-songs. The general banter at football. Not too many interested in the match result as such. It was a testimonial for Keith 'Rhino' Stevens that was probably doubling as a pre-season friendly, too, although it was fairly competitive. One of those games that passed by in a haze.

After the match, you may only have one chance to get at an escort. The police would want to wrap them up and get them out of the area. They were escorted out of the North Stand, through the Silwood estate and on to Rotherhithe New Road. We attacked them there. At that stage, the numbers were fairly even, probably a couple of hundred each, and a big mêlée ensued at the front. Spurs came off worst and they ran. We chased them down to Surrey Quays where they tried to make another stand. They were no match for us and were taking a severe beating. We had them pinned down, and again the Old Bill split us up.

We cut through Southwark Park and a mob of us were there when a Spurs boy jumped over the wall, obviously trying to get away from someone – right into us. One fella punched him. He was trying to fight back and both were throwing punches. Bang. Our boy caught him with a good 'un and the geezer hit the floor. The punch that dropped him was flush on the chin. He got stamped on, right on the head. Stamp … stamp. His head was bouncing off the grass. He was out. He was left there.

We moved on to get to their main firm again and attacked them from the side. This caught them by total surprise. We had armed ourselves with lumps of wood, bottles and bricks. They were taking a severe beating. They didn't know what had hit them and were hiding behind police cars. The Old Bill were running around like headless chickens initially. After a while, they did regain control by following the retreating Spurs firm and getting in between the two sets of fans. Spurs had come down to take on the big boys; they were no match.

That night one of the stupidest things I have ever heard happened. Some Spurs led by Trevor 'The Spanner' Tanner, Tottenham's own south-east London boy, returned to the scene of their humiliation. They smashed up The Caulkers, a little quiet pub with a couple of old boys having a peaceful Saturday night booze-up. You would have thought they would have known there wouldn't be any Millwall in that pub. Hmm …

maybe that was why they chose that pub. Just a thought.

Going back to the late Sixties, there was one FA Cup tie with Spurs when we were expecting a huge invasion from north London. We were drinking in the Old Kent Road before the game, keeping an eye out for any Spurs. With nothing happening, we walked to the ground. We were in Monson Road when I saw a few fellas I knew from the Walworth Road, about ten of them going toe-to-toe with an even-sized number of Spurs. About five of us broke into a sprint. As we came into the side of them, I pulled out my truncheon. Bang. I hit one straight across the side of the face. This knocked him back into his mate. It seemed to rattle them, and we started to get the upper hand. Now a few of them were on the deck and, seeing this, the rest ran. We did not give chase; they'd had enough.

We moved off towards the ground. I spoke to the fellas I knew and they had heard these geezers saying they had bashed up some Millwall fans, so they got stuck into them. The match was a 0–0 draw, a good result for us. I missed the replay due to a run-in with the law.

29

WITHIN A STONE'S THROW – CHARLTON AND CRYSTAL PALACE

W ho?
Some clubs are just too insignificant, aren't they?

30
ROAD TO NOWHERE

The match against Swansea in February 2001 had been moved to an early kick-off, having been regarded by the authorities as another of our 'potentially explosive' games. They were right on that one. We hired a minibus. One of the lads had organised it with about 20 of us in it. We all chipped in and the hope, obviously, was that we were going to avoid the main police escort for as long as possible. We could do whatever we wanted, and all met up at the Elephant & Castle. Everyone was there with a crate under their arms, a couple of grams of charlie, and a few were carrying their weapons of choice – coshes, hammers, Stanley knives, Coke, beers, tools. Twenty Millwall. Some combination. We piled into the minibus and we were away, across London and on to the A4 leading all the way to the Severn Bridge.

We had probably been in the van for a couple of hours when we had a call that the Old Bill were pulling coaches over near the border. We made a decision that we were going to turn around. There were enough weapons on the bus to start a war. We told the driver to take the next exit and head back to Swindon, which was the biggest town we had passed. A couple more phone calls told us what was happening with the coaches.

The police were looking for any reason to nick people and stop them going any further. They were pulling them all to pieces with sniffer dogs and full search teams. If the weaponry and drug sniffer dogs had come on our coach, they would have gone off their heads.

We arrived in Swindon, found a pub on the outskirts and spent the next couple of hours drinking and getting reports from the others who had made it by train. They told us that the Old Bill had them under wraps from start to finish. Inside the ground, it was a bit lively but there was no chance of getting at Swansea with the police presence. We were gutted we never got to Swansea but at least we had outmanoeuvred the Old Bill.

We stayed in Swindon and had a good drink-up until well into the night. A right unusual day, really. But maybe the police had a bit of intelligence or something that day. Fair play to them. Luckily for us, we had a bit of intelligence ourselves and, rather than risk any or all of us getting nicked, we U-turned to Swindon and had a right good laugh.

Thinking back, why no one suggested, 'Let's do all our cocaine now,' I don't know. Someone may have followed with, 'Then let's just throw the hammers, coshes and knives out the window.' And finally someone could have said, 'Then let's just go there.' I don't know. But logic in a van filled with 20 booze-fuelled, cocaine-addled Millwall football hooligans with menace on their minds is a priceless commodity. Well, it was on that day. I suppose, in their defence, some had their weapons with them.

Myself, I never carried one but some of the boys treated theirs like pets. 'Well, why not stash them and pick them up on the way back?' OK, we were all fucked on coke, beer and bad thoughts. Swindon was safe. For now.

31
ROCK BOTTOM

L ast game of the 1995/96 season. It was never going to be trouble with Ipswich, but it was a good turnout. We had to win to be in with a chance of survival and, even if we did, we still weren't guaranteed to stay up. About 50 of us met at London Bridge and threw a few beers down our necks in Garfunkel's at the station. Heading over to Liverpool Street, we were all in good spirits, full of confidence and hope. On the football special to Ipswich, the beer was flowing.

We arrived having had a good booze-up and a snort of Charlie; a fine start to the day. A few thousand of us were milling around the station. You felt the police presence but not the massive police operations of future years. We walked to the ground and I felt supercharged. We got into the ground no problem. A great atmosphere, with everyone bouncing. As the game went on, it was getting more and more jittery and it became clear we needed to win.

The Ipswich fans were mocking us with chants of 'Going down, going down'. It finished 0–0 in front of over 17,000 fans. We *were* going down. Fucking hell. Christmas we were on top and May we were down. Fucking football is a killer at times.

The atmosphere turned and a fun, jovial day out was going to go off now. Seats were getting smashed and thrown on to the pitch. People were going mental everywhere.

We tried to get at the Ipswich fans in the home end first. No joy. The Old Bill saw to that as a mob of about 30 of us tried to leave the stadium. No way did they want any 'Wall outside just yet, but I blasted my way through and, on leaving the ground, was intent on doing damage. Utter menace in my mind. The taunting and goading of the Ipswich fans that hadn't mattered at the start now mattered. We were charged up and someone was going to be on the end of something. I was going to make sure of that. There was a mob of about 50 Ipswich fans 30ft away and I was gunning straight for them. They were standing their ground and waving us forward. We were only half their number as all the others were still inside.

As I was heading for them, someone grabbed me from behind and yanked me by my coat collar. It choked and jarred me, so instinctively I spun around and swung a big left hook. Bang. Right on the geezer's jaw. He dropped to the floor, letting go of my collar. Fuck! Something hard hit me on the back of the head. I turned slightly and threw a punch in the general direction of my attacker; as I did, someone else jumped on my back before more piled in, pinning me to the floor. I was well and truly nicked. They dragged me up and quickly bundled me into a nearby police van. The doors slammed shut. A little word to myself: 'Stay calm, no point kicking off in here, you're not going to escape.' It is, after all, our right to remain silent. There was none of that 'rights' stuff, just bundled into a van. Law unto themselves, really. Surely they are supposed to read us our rights?

I was still a bit stunned because I hadn't actually realised it was the police arresting me to begin with. I only noticed it was a steward as the big left hook was mid-swing. No pulling out at that stage. He was copping for one. Fucking stewards being heroes. Two more were thrown into the van. I recognised their faces but they were not with our boys; they were part of a different firm. No great conversations in the van with the other two chaps, other than a few unpleasantries aimed at the Suffolk Constabulary. You never know who has ears on you in situations like that. So not too much is ever spoken.

The van sped back to the local nick and we were led to the desk to be searched and booked – the usual bollocks. As I was at the desk, a plain-clothed copper came up to me and said, 'We've got you now, you cunt.'

I just laughed. 'Fuck off, you mug.'

I was read my rights, processed and expected to be interviewed on the Sunday. It was Saturday evening and they would have their hands full with Millwall in town.

After being placed in a cell on my own, the doctor was sent to see me. So I was taken from the cell by one copper to an interview room. The doctor looked me over, checked for concussion, looked in my eyes and scanned the cut on my head. It was a full-blooded cosh to the back of the head and it had done some damage. Be under no illusions, they weren't doing this shit for my benefit. They were only making sure the people they have arrested are not going to keel over on them. It is to cover their own arses after using force. I was taken back to the cell after a couple of minutes and I could then start to make myself comfortable. The Old Bill had kindly left me with my cigarettes but had taken my lighter. They love to play their little mind games. So I just got my head down – no watch, no phone, no lighter, belt taken off me, but they left my shoelaces in. I think they realised I was never going to be on suicide watch. Time to sleep.

It was hard to tell how much later I got woken up. It was time for my interview. The Old Bill walking me to the interview room gave me a right pile of old shite. 'Just give us some info, what went on, we'll get you processed and get you out of here, probably won't be no charge.'

'OK, no problem,' I replied.

I was taken into an interview room with two coppers. The tape was put on. One said the time and date and introduced himself and the other copper. He asked if I could confirm my name.

'No comment.'

Don't remember one single question after that, wasn't interested in anything he was saying, just listened for the drone of his voice to finish. When it was silent – 'No comment,' 'No comment,' 'No comment.'

Funny. Remember everything I said but cannot remember anything they said. It probably lasted about ten minutes before they realised they weren't going to get anywhere. With both sides really sick of it, they took me back to the cell. Having paid that little attention I did not even hear the time at the beginning or the end. 'Interview started at ...' 'Interview terminated at ...' It was time to go back to the cell. Back to sleep.

I got woken up again, only this time with some sausage, fried egg, bacon and a little spoonful of beans. No drink. It was passed through the hatch but it did not matter what was on that plate. It was never going to be eaten. Why? I did not trust them and was sure they would have spat on it or put something in it. It may have been a little cocaine paranoia but in absolute sobriety I would have done the same thing.

'Here's your breakfast.'

'You may as well take that back ... any chance of a Chinese?'

Just a grunt came back. Obviously, I wasn't expecting them

to run out and get me a takeaway. He left. I got my head down again with no problem. We had done some heavy drinking and been snorting charlie so it was only what I would have been doing anyway. Bit of a cunt with the cigarettes and fucking starving, but totally determined not to eat any of the shite that they put in front of me. Sleep was my friend. Having woken up on my own the next time, I hit the buzzer and got an Old Bill at the cell door.

'What's going on? When am I getting out of here?'

'You ain't ... you're going to court on Monday.'

'Any chance of a Chinese?'

I half expected that at this stage. Tough to call exactly how long but I was sure it had been over 24 hours since they put me in the cell. No lunch was offered. No dinner was offered. I buzzed them again.

'Any chance of a drop of water?'

'Yes, OK.'

Took the water off him. 'Any chance of a Chinese?'

The usual grunt. Got my head back down and slept for a while. Then the same scenario. Woke up and buzzed him. 'Any chance of any water?'

'OK.'

He brought it, I took it and asked, 'That Chinese turned up yet?'

Grunt.

You go into a bit of a brain shut-down. Think as little as possible and sleep as much as possible. I knew court was looming on Monday. The cell was warm enough with a blue, plastic-covered type of piss-proof mattress and a grubby old blanket. We weren't in The Ritz here and beggars can't be choosers. It was comfortable enough and luckily I am a good sleeper.

On the Sunday night after hearing court was imminent, I used my telephone call to bell my brief. After pleasantries, I informed him of the situation. 'I've been nicked at football, up in Suffolk Court on Monday.'

'OK, OK ... we'll have somebody there for you.'

End of conversation. Went back to the cell and got my head down no problem.

Half awake and half asleep came the rattle of the keys, a bang on the cell and the door was opened. No breakfast had been offered. Cuffed and taken straight out and into a van. A couple of other fellas in the van were on their way to court, too. No conversation. Not even a hello. Did not want to be embroiled in a conversation with strangers, just wanted to stay in my own little world. Keeping focused on what to say but bracing myself for the worst. I was not 100 per cent sure but it was no good thinking, 'Only got a few hours to go here.' Think the worst and anything else is a bonus then.

Got out of the van at Suffolk Magistrates' Court. Just another characterless, soulless, heartless, cold, shitty environment. Back into the holding cells before meeting with the brief. Still cuffed, they took me to another room. He already had a bit of paperwork, including the charge sheet – common assault and affray – and my statement: 'No comment.' Times ten or more. After the pleasantries, he asked me a couple of questions.

'So can you tell me exactly what happened?'

'I came out the football, there was a bit of to-ing and fro-ing, a bit of argy-bargy, someone hit me from behind ... so I hit them back ... next thing I know, I had been hit over the head with something ... next thing I know, I've come around in a police van.'

'Oh, so you were assaulted?'

'Yes, obviously!'

'And, in self-defence, you have tried to defend yourself?'

'Yes. I was assaulted and defended myself.'

'Well, OK, I can do something with that. Did you see the doctor?'

'Yes.'

'OK, leave it with me, I'll go and speak with the Prosecution and pick up the doctor's report.'

I was taken back to the holding cell, still handcuffed and still without food. Fortunately at that stage, food is the last thing that you are thinking about. I sat in there on my own for another hour or so. The other two fellas had gone, probably first up in court. After a while, the Old Bill took me back to the same room. My brief was sat there.

'Right, cut a little deal, plead guilty on a public order offence. Because of your injuries, we've got the common assault and affray dropped. Plead guilty and we'll have it wrapped up today. Expect a small custodial sentence but I'll push for community service or bound over to keep the peace.'

In my mind, I was thinking, an hour ago I could have been looking at a couple of years maybe, now it is only a couple of months. Do half and out in four weeks. Happy days. Now I just wanted to get it over and done.

Still in handcuffs, the Old Bill escorted me back to the holding cell. Another hour passed and another Old Bill came in, finally un-cuffed me after about five hours, and led me upstairs into the dock. A quick scan around. Big Queen's crest was the first thing I noticed, then the Bench, the dock, my brief and the Prosecution. No witnesses. The court usher, me and my guard. That was it. The three magistrates came in.

'All rise.' Everyone stood up.

The magistrate in the middle gave my name and address, then he asked, 'Can you confirm your name and address?'

'Yes.'

'How do you plead?'

'Guilty.'

He carried on with a bit of writing on his sheet. My brief stood up. His words in the whole court process were a bit of a blur. I had not eaten since Saturday morning and, in my head, I was preparing to go down. All that was going to make any impact at this stage was the sentence.

I vaguely remember him saying stuff like 'we are pleading guilty ... hope the court takes this into consideration'.

The Prosecution stood up and made my day. 'We are not looking for a custodial sentence.'

My heart lifted.

'But we are looking for a banning order.'

At that stage, that was a good deal and a fine trade. He sat down. The three magistrates trudged off for a chat. At one stage, my brief came over. 'I think we will be all right here.' He walked away and the three magistrates returned.

'All rise.'

The sentence: 100 hours' community service – 'OK,' I am thinking; bound over for one year to keep the peace – 'Fair enough,' I am thinking; three-year ban from all stadia – 'Fucking bollocks,' I am thinking! All stadia! England games, everything. No football for three years. Shite. We had Euro '96 kicking off in a few weeks.

I shook the hand of my brief, a good job well done. Walked out the court and back to the police station to pick up my stuff. It was time to get the fuck out of this one-horse town and I headed back to London in a great mood. I'd worry about the sentence later.

The effects of my sentence? One hundred hours' community service – painting a school in Southwark. Seven hours a day on a Saturday in the first few weeks, then it started on a Tuesday, too. Before the new season had kicked off, the community service was done. The school had a new lick of paint when the kids returned from the summer holidays. My pleasure.

And I was bound over to keep the peace, so I steered clear of Old Bill for a year and attempted to keep my nose clean. Just made sure I didn't get caught. No great shakes.

As for the three-year banning order, it went from easy to tough to easy again. Obviously, all the Euro '96 games were included. At that early stage, there was no way I was risking a visit to Wembley. Fuck that. The Old Bill were out in force during the tournament and my well-known face was now banned. Instead, we went on the piss for every single England game and had a ball, like the whole nation believing Skinner and Baddiel singing 'It's Coming Home'. Steering well clear of Wembley and the temptation of hearing 'Tickets … spare tickets …' Remember thinking to myself that if we got to the final, I wouldn't be missing that. Didn't know whether to laugh or cry after Gareth Southgate missed his pen.

The first Millwall game of the ban was Wrexham. It was the start of the new season and our first game back in the third tier of English football. At kick-off, my lips were wrapped around a pint of beer and my nose was stuck in a bag of charlie. Right up until the boys left at quarter-to-three, it was a normal match day, the only difference being, I didn't go to the match and stayed in the pub when everyone made their way to The Den. There were a handful of drinkers to keep me company and the football was on the television. The boys taking the piss on the way out was the hardest part. Time flies on cocaine and, after a couple of little snorts, they all came bouncing in again. There was no trouble that day. If one of the boys had burst in the pub shouting, 'It's kicking off on Ilderton Road,' then one hooligan with a banning order would have been involved.

The ban came into force in May and, by October, around 15 Millwall games had come and gone. The choice now was either to start picking and choosing matches or to continue with the banning order. It was time to pick and choose. I was looking for the games where I knew there would be trouble, making it easier not to be spotted as the Old Bill would have their hands full. By this time, of course, my face was well known to the police.

The first game back was on Wednesday, 29 October against Bristol City at home. The following week we played Fulham at home. Banned man was in attendance. Didn't want to push my luck, so I kept away until a mob of us went for a jolly up at Southend away in January. Went to the last game of the season, undecided as to what to do the following season. My mind was made up when Theo installed Billy Bonds as manager and came out with loads of shite about shirt colour and crests. Banned boy would be going to every game and venting his feelings. That season and the next, I carried on going to football as normal, completely ignoring the ban.

Was I worried? Cautious more than worried. I had changed my hairstyle from longish hair to a skinhead and was sitting in the quiet part of the ground at the first few games. In the 1998/99 season, the ban never entered my head. It had been an inconvenience more than any tangible threat of being arrested while banned. The first league game at home was spent in the normal way at one of our regular pubs. If trouble had occurred that day, then my involvement was a given. Banning orders do not stop hooligans from hooliganism. Granted, it stopped me going to the game for a while, but not for long. As for being back looking for trouble, I hadn't gone away.

Ipswich, last game of the season, was a bad day for me and Millwall. We got relegated after being top of the league before Christmas and I got put in a cell all weekend at 6.00pm after flying on a Saturday morning. Mick McCarthy was our gaffer when we were top and he was sounded out to take over the Republic of Ireland job when Jack Charlton retired. McCarthy just gave up then and waited for his new post. It triggered a tragic series of events that culminated in Millwall being relegated and me being apprehended. So I blame Mick McCarthy.

32
SHEEP IN WOLVES' CLOTHING

We left London Euston at a very early hour on 31 October 2001, after meeting in the station pub as pre-arranged. The concern was that the British Transport Police could have tipped off the Met or the West Midlands Police. A couple of quick pints to get everyone together and we set off for Wolves. It was time to pay The Subway Army a visit. Our aim was to avoid being escorted to the ground, hoping the Old Bill were going to be surprised by our early start and not be 100 per cent organised.

Around 200 of us arrived at Wolverhampton station. There was a police presence as we came out of the station, but certainly not enough to hold 200 of our main boys. Everyone from our firm had turned up, around 30–40 of us. The rest were made up of about 4–5 other firms/factions like us, 20–30-strong mini-firms. They can come in any size or number, some turn up in groups of six, some in fours, some two-handed and some just on their own. It was most definitely around 200 of Millwall's main firm. And we were ready for a ruck.

As we came out of the station, we spotted a large group of The Subway Army. The Wolves firm were drinking in The Feathers pub. We had been hoping for this. Straight away, I knew the police had no fucking chance of containing us. The excitement was on. No time for discussions, but I could see others in our firm whose adrenalin was pumping as much as mine.

Without hesitation, we smashed past the police presence and attacked them. We were heading for their pub and there was, in effect, no police escort. I was running at their pub. The Subway Army had a fair few outside and they started to ready themselves for our attack, picking up glasses and bottles and bracing themselves for the first exchanges.

The ones at the front steamed straight into them, punching and kicking. A few Wolves boys hit the floor. Hard to count, but certainly a few and certainly enough to send The Subway Army straight into the pub. The ones on the floor took a right good kicking. None of them out cold, but a few went into the foetal position before scrambling up and running in the pub themselves. Not one person has got team colours on in this situation. No reds versus blues here, and you can always miss things going on in a crowd scene. The exchanges lasted less than 30 seconds – 30 seconds of absolute mayhem and pandemonium. All The Subway Army scuttled back into their pub. None of our boys went in, but Wolves took a good hiding. Two of their boys were slashed.

When that happens, someone has maybe pulled a cut-throat out and given a quick whip like an old barber, or punched with a Stanley sticking out of his hand. Maybe someone's been hit by a bottle. I didn't find out until the next day in the Sunday papers. It goes back to the old Millwall way. No one goes around after a bit of a ruck saying, 'I done this and I done that.' You are only one boast away from an arrest, after all.

Wolves hadn't put up much resistance and sought sanctuary inside the pub. The Old Bill restored order by surrounding the pub and saved them from more punishment. Those at the very front and involved do not want to get nicked. They would run through our crowd and create a sort of suction – they'd fade into our boys and one and all would turn. Within minutes, the Old Bill had mobilised and the reinforcements arrived – police on horseback, dogs, vans, riot squad. They had been prepared. We are Millwall and quite well known after all, but we had caught them with their pants down. Our tactic of getting the early train had paid off. The Wolves Subway Army took a bit of a kicking.

The rest of the journey to the ground was under a heavy police escort. After the game, it was the same. Surrounded with a heavy escort back to the station and back to Euston. Get us the fuck away from the ground and get us the fuck out of their city. You can tell on some cops' faces they have the fear, but some others love it. They can hide behind the badge and do what the fuck they want. Those on the power trip get as much fun out of it as us.

33

HOOLIGANS IN YOUR LIVING ROOM

If anyone wonders why we were filmed in another documentary, we only have to listen to the description of Millwall by undercover journalist Jason Williams in October 2002: 'By far the most dangerous football firm in Britain.'

I cannot help but wonder if the timing of this documentary was in any way linked to what I have described as 'the mad season'. From August 2001 to May 2002, it seemed we were in the press as regular as clockwork. Was it all that mad, or was it just usual football banter, a bit of rucking, a bit of aggro with the Old Bill and all just vastly more publicised? Let us assume for a moment that the BBC have commissioned a documentary on, ooh, let's say football hooliganism. They know it is a ten-month project. Could it be beyond the powers of a corporation like the BBC to drip-feed the public a diet of hooligan stories about Millwall culminating in the crescendo of their own documentary? Is that an impossibility? Is that unfeasible?

When you examine the events closely, some startling facts appear – like the match against Spurs in August 2001. A pre-season friendly and we caught the Old Bill on the hop. It was well arranged. After that came Birmingham away and we were wrapped up all day. Cardiff and Burnley at home in the space of a few days and young Millwall have a bit of fun with the riot police. Late evening sun with beers in hand. Nothing too major. Forest was the same. At Wolves away, we beat the Old Bill by travelling early, a little ruck with Wolves and it was game over. Portsmouth in December at home, they came for a ruck, they took a pasting and went home. Nothing major – except all of them were heavily reported. Then one of the biggest headline-grabbers came at home to Birmingham in January 2002: 'A half-eaten pie thrown at the linesman.'

Some geezer with his Christmas turkey still clogging his arteries and fresh on his tastebuds flung a sweaty steak pie and how the press loved it. Forest and Portsmouth away, Sheffield Wednesday and Wolves at home, we were heavily policed which prevented any real trouble at all these games. Didn't prevent big headlines from following Millwall, though. So the documentary was aired. And what happened? The Birmingham riot. We had just been knocked out of the play-offs. Does life imitate art? Think we all know the answer to that non-riddle.

So what of the documentary itself? The journalist involved made some interesting remarks: 'Filming undercover – whether it is exposing disreputable businessmen or mixing with hooligan gangs – can be exciting, but also very dangerous.' So, there is the BBC journalist admitting to the kicks he was getting by running with Millwall. 'Exciting because of the complete adrenalin rushes it gives you and dangerous because of the fear of exposure.' Yes. That just about sums it up for us, too, Jason. I like this guy.

'Months of hard work and research could be wasted if you fail to convince someone you are who they think you are. There is also the threat of being the victim of a violent attack.' Not sure about months but certainly a bit of planning is involved nowadays. As for being the victim? Concentrate. Hit. Don't get hit. Hit. Don't get hit. Come on now, Jason, get with the programme.

'There is a fascination among football hooligans with designer labels such as Lacoste, Burberry, Aquascutum and, in particular, with Italian label Stone Island.' *Fashionistas* they are, Jason. All the gear with no idea.

'Having trawled the designer shops, I felt confident that I would at least be accepted as a "lad" – a term football hooligans use amongst their peers.' Nice one, Jason lad. Welcome to this wonderful world of ours. A sub-culture with a buzz you can't buy.

'But in my opinion, by far the most dangerous football firm in Britain is Millwall. I have travelled undercover to eight matches, home and away, with them this season.' Why thanks very much, Jason lad. Only confirming what the whole country already knew.

'In March 2002, we were expecting trouble at their game in Portsmouth. Earlier in the season, I had witnessed a mob of Millwall lads attack a Pompey fan outside The New Den in south-east London.' More hoping than expecting, Jason. You know the term 'bubble wrapped'?

'Walking to the ground I could see that many of Millwall's hardcore hooligans had made the trip. They are known as The Bushwackers, and they had not come all this way to take in the sea air.' He was right; most of the top boys were there. But we do like the seaside games to get a bit of clean air into our smog-filled lungs. So wrong on that one, lad.

'Stewards were searching everyone entering the ground. I became concerned for my safety.' Wise move. You would have been on very thin ice if you had been outed in the middle of the firm. In serious jeopardy.

'I have been searched by police officers and stewards before. Trying to explain who you are and why you are carrying a secret camera tends to lead to a lot of questioning. The last thing I wanted was to be searched in front of Millwall's mob. Casually, I moved to the back, and slipped away down a side road before the police had an opportunity to usher everyone into the ground. I waited until kick-off, as by then the stewards and police were inside. I paid my entrance fee and walked through the turnstile. Another close escape.' It was that.

Jason did make some very valid and interesting points. Notably: 'With the huge amounts of money now involved in the football industry, the role of branding and marketing has become central to the national game. Anything that is seen to present a negative image of football is very unwelcome.'

He discovered how far underground hooliganism was, at least in the eyes of the football authorities. During the making of his programme, he approached a number of clubs and footballing authorities to contribute. The Football Association refused him permission to use any footage of football matches. They stated that their responsibilities involved 'maintaining and promoting a positive image for football'. Perhaps Jason was more surprised by their response than by anything else that he discovered. Except, of course, for the buzz he found himself having with us. He also said Millwall declined to take part in the programme.

'Despite the extraordinary scenes of violence and disorder we filmed involving Millwall hooligans, the club preferred not to be interviewed.' Now that surely came as no surprise. Nobody really wants to acknowledge or even think about the rat in their kitchen.

'They claim to have taken a lot of action against the hooligans who tarnish the image of the club, but still preferred not to contribute to our film.' Ah, Jason. They try at the club. They do but, as you discovered, we are a hardy bunch of boys and, on occasions, the runaway train will not be stopped.

Cardiff City apparently set stringent conditions on appearing in the programme, conditions that apparently no broadcaster could comply with. They also claimed that the BBC was on a crusade against Welsh football. He had been with us to Cardiff, so he must have seen that one coming. Fucking typically touchy there, the old Cardiffians. He then approached Stoke City.

'Another club with a very problematic hooligan following, and a club which has gone to great lengths to combat the problem – including a joint initiative with Port Vale called True Supporters Against Violence. Stoke, too, preferred not to appear in the series.' Jesus, Jason. Pattern emerging here. You sure it wasn't just your aftershave? You been buying the cheap stuff down the market? Or was your patter slightly flawed? You must have got someone to talk to you. Finally, he got word – Bristol City was an exception to the rule.

'Their Chief Executive, Colin Sextone, told us about the appalling scenes at the match in Cardiff and was frank enough to admit to the role of Bristol City hooligans in some of the trouble.' So finally, and surprisingly, one goes on the record and admits guilt. See, Jason, as you know, all that the football authorities and clubs will do is deny, deny, deny. Why? Hooliganism now seldom occurs inside the ground, so as far as clubs are concerned it's job done. Over to you, local constabulary. That is what we pay you for. Extortionate amounts, too. Such that Wigan Chairman Dave Whelan nearly took his beloved club down over the bill he was receiving from the police. They threatened to prevent any games being played, in effect shutting him down. He paid. The police and the State know billions are kicking around and they want their slice of the football pie. Clubs don't want to acknowledge hooliganism because it is costly enough, without the fines on top of that already paid to the Old Bill. The Premier League doesn't want to acknowledge the problem because it doesn't want to tarnish the brand from its clean-cut image. Remember Tiger Woods after his infidelities? Sponsors can be fickle. The FA is the same. Politicians don't want to acknowledge it as they claim to have virtually conquered it. So hooliganism is pushed around the plate like a scabby sirloin at a vegetarian's dinner. Everyone wants to pass it to each other, no one knows what the fuck to do with it and they have no idea where the bin is. Hooliganism remains.

Not sure what exactly this documentary exposed. If it showed Jason anything, he learnt how much of a buzz it was to run with the Millwall mob. Welcome to my world. That's a wrap!

34

BANGING THE BRUM

The rivalry with Birmingham goes back a long way. Our hatred probably started from the 1971/72 season. On the last day of the season, we beat Preston 2–0. News was coming in that Birmingham had lost to Sheffield Wednesday, sparking wild scenes of celebration. We thought we were finally promoted to the top flight of football after 77 years in the lower leagues; the Promised Land had actually been reached. This news turned out to be untrue. Birmingham got the result they needed to take our place as one of the promoted teams. One idiot with a transistor radio and a warped sense of humour would be my guess. Terrace tittle-tattle spreads like wildfire, like a Mexican wave of whispers: 'Birmingham have lost – we're up!'

This was enough to breed a deep-rooted dislike of all things Birmingham in the minds of many Millwall. Football is mad. We know this.

In 1987, we were in The Fox after a good 3–1 win over Birmingham. We were playing well. Two coaches full of their fans pulled up outside the pub. They were stuck in the London traffic. After spotting us they started with the hand gestures and 'come on' signals. So we obliged and steamed out on to the road. They were now sitting ducks. The buses were pelted with bottles, glasses and bricks. All the windows of the coaches were smashed. They finally managed to move off when the traffic moved forward, saving the Birmingham fans inside from a severe beating. I later spoke to some of my mates that were drinking in The Crown and Anchor and they said that the coaches had gone past them giving 'wanker' signs out of the window, probably not realising they would soon be stuck in the London traffic outside a Millwall pub. Fools.

We have always thought that, as a firm, they're game at home but they've never really done anything at Millwall. Their claim to be a top-five firm is a bit of a joke. They seem to do well against second-rate firms but come up short against the top firms. If you asked people across the country their top five hooligan firms, I don't think they would make it. Maybe in a top ten. Maybe. They have come and had a little go without any success. On one occasion in The New Den, they brought a decent crowd. We were sitting in the West Stand Upper. The first half was incident-free. As the second half started, we heard the shouts: 'Zulus ... Zulus ... fuckin' come on, Millwall!'

They came running up the stairs and across the seats, about 20 of them. We had the same number and steamed into them. The first two at the front got put on their arses. The rest turned and ran back down the stairs into the concourse. We chased and caught up with them. The main ones at the front were getting a good kicking on the floor. More Zulus came up the stairs. The first one reached the top and someone stepped forward and hit him with probably one of the best punches I have ever seen. He hit the deck like his legs had been chopped off. Seeing this, the rest fled back down the stairs.

It was reported in the *Mail on Sunday* the next day that one Birmingham fan was hospitalised with a dislocated shoulder. That must have been him at the top of the stairs when he hit the deck. He was fucked up. Fair play to them, they came looking for us. Again, they took a bit of a pasting. One consolation for the dislocated shoulder boy, though, several more Birmingham fans joined him in the hospital after the second altercation. Funnily enough, as also reported in the *Sunday Mail*.

So on to 2 May 2002. Stern-John scored in a 1–0 win which sent Birmingham to the final in Cardiff on the back of a 2–1 aggregate triumph. It was enough to trigger national headlines: 'SHOULD MILLWALL FANS BE BANNED? ... Fans of Millwall could be barred from away matches following the rioting which left nearly 50 police officers injured.'

Chairman Theo Paphitis apologised for the mayhem and the club said it would consider 'placing restrictions on travelling supporters, both home and away, and rescheduling kick-off times and dates of matches'.

A joint statement from the police and the club said: 'The club has offered their fullest support to the post-incident investigation and has pledged that anything that can be done to identify those responsible for the violence will be done.'

It was the First Division play-off semi-final second leg and Birmingham scored in the last minute. Devastating. Gutted. After getting a great draw up there in the first leg we were sure our final place was booked. Watching the Zulus victoriously taunting us from the away end was too much for too many. We could not beat them on the pitch but we were going to try and salvage something good from this disastrous night. We made our way round to the away end and started to congregate on the corner of Ilderton and Zampa Road, looking to get at the Zulus. We were due a proper ruck with them.

What happened next was probably one of the biggest fuck-ups made by the Old Bill against a football firm. They made the mistake of instigating trouble. Instead of just blocking the way to the away end, they charged us with batons. We weren't starting any trouble or even trying to break police lines. Of course, we wanted to kick fuck out of the Zulus but they had the whole of Zampa Road blocked. We would never have got past them and were just hanging around. That one badly misjudged decision to charge us sparked one of the largest riots seen at an English football game.

See, they were so used to baton-charging students and pensioners who could not pay their poll tax. One of the May Day marchers, Mick Gordon, said, 'I'm appalled at the behaviour of the police in this situation. They seem to be turning this peaceful protest into a potentially dangerous situation.' Met Chief Sir John Stevens has admitted that each officer had their own individual sprays of CS gas and they all had plastic bullets. Zero tolerance is here to stay.

Still, bit of a different ball game when they charged us. We all turned and ran at first, of course. Fucking brutal sight watching rows of Robocops running at you with coshes locked and loaded. And they were getting their rocks off on that first charge at us – no doubt in my mind. They were ducking and diving themselves, though, after we had lobbed a load of debris at them and charged back. No doubt about that either. We weren't going to throw a pension book or an essay at them in reply.

So why did they charge? They had a new man at the helm who wanted to show he was Charlie Big Spuds to his new force and take the Millwall mob down. Perhaps they were just bored. Did they want to break in all their shiny new coshes? Maybe it was all about retribution. They are like that, the Old Bill. There had been a few other skirmishes earlier in the season where they did not have a good day. Like all teams do in the last game of the season, they wanted to go out on a high. All summer to relax then.

Police are there for crowd control, not crowd attack. I would love to be able to say we wound them up and they fell for it. We never; they just went for it. Some crazy bastards underneath them visors. Bet you half of them are running with some firm on their Saturday off.

After the first charge, we had returned with our own missiles. It caused the Old Bill to fall back to Zampa Road. This back and forth continued for about 20 minutes before the cavalry arrived. The mounted police come charging into us. Fireworks, literally. We let them off under the horses causing them to panic and run in all directions. Obviously, something completely alien to the Old Bill – usually charging in with horses would be enough to control any crowd. With their trump card taken away, they had no way to control us. Every time they charged, they were met by a barrage of missiles and fireworks and were taking heavy casualties. After each attack, they were in disarray. Cars were set on fire in Verneys Road causing them even more problems because of the smoke.

We moved into The Bramcote Arms in the middle of the Bonamy estate and just continued what we had been doing. The Old Bill came near us and each time they came under attack from everything we could get our hands on – bricks, glasses and more fireworks. The police had really come unstuck on a night when they had started the trouble. With us at the pub, any attempts to move us on came to nothing.

Our attention now turned to the Birmingham fans. We were in touch with a few of them by phone and could see the escort in Ilderton Road; we had a go at getting to them but ended up fighting with the Old Bill. We contacted the Brum fans on the phone to get them to make a break from the escort. They were not interested. Another poor show from Birmingham.

The fighting with the police had now moved to the corner of Rotherhithe New Road and Ilderton Road, past South Bermondsey train station. With us now past the station it allowed them to get Birmingham in and away. Once we knew Birmingham had gone, things fizzled out. All in all, this had gone on for two hours. It was a shame we never got to the Zulus that night. We had a good firm ready for it. With the heavy casualties the police took, I bet they wished they had let us have a go at them. There were 70 police officers and horses injured that night.

One Old Bill veteran of the May Day and Poll Tax riots said, 'The rampage on this night outside Millwall Football Club was the worst violence I have ever experienced.'

Sergeant Russell Lamb was one of their 47 officers injured in the clashes after our defeat. He was quoted as saying that the situation was 'like a battlefield ...' with other Old Bill '... dropping like nine-pins'. He went on to tell of how he and other police '... endured two hours ... of ridiculous and mindless violence' at the hands of hundreds of our firm. 'It was one of the most frightening situations I have ever been in ...' Fair comment, I would say. It was fucking crazy.

Apparently, he had served 15 years with the Metropolitan Police at the time. So you would guess that he had seen a few frightening situations. Think it shows how much we were provoked by the police on the night, if the truth be told. They never learn. We had just gone out at the semi-final stage. Again. And they thought the best policy for them was to charge us. For fuck's sake. You have got a lot of hyped-up, pissed-off, pissed-up Millwall milling around here. Not particularly intimidated by the Old Bill at the best of times, as they should know. Let alone on a night like this one. That was just like waving a red rag to an angry, rabid, hungry, just-been-knocked-out-in-the-semis bull. Not the wisest manoeuvre.

Lamb reckoned about 900 Millwall left the ground intent on trouble after the game. Not a bad guess from him. I had it at about 1,000 myself. 'We are evil' was definitely true on this night, and particularly once we had been provoked. Mr Lamb continued '... officers were falling over in pain ... the crowd were laughing at the officers. They were laughing in their faces and taunting them.' Not one Millwall who was there would deny that. We were laughing! This same sergeant needed seven stitches in his chin after being hit by a lump of concrete the size of a cricket ball. He also suffered a foot and knee injury. That decision to charge wasn't so clever now, eh! He probably had about ten weeks off on fully paid sick leave.

'One of my colleagues' visors was split in two when a brick hit it ... you could not believe the amount of debris ... every single car had a brick on the back seat, concrete had been thrown through windscreens and sunroofs.' Not all deliberately. Some of our boys can't half throw a punch and kick, but they can't throw a rock or a brick. Like everyone else that gets quoted after a night like this, he was shocked, stunned and upset that a football match could result in such violence. Funny that, because myself and a lot of the people I spoke with felt that it was not the football match that created the level of violence but your police tactic of charging the Millwall fans that acted as the catalyst. Of course, you will never read that in any of the papers the next day. He also felt sadness for all the local people that woke up to the mess the following morning. 'The people in this area go to work to pay for their possessions.' What area doesn't? But not a bad attempt at police PR to get the locals on their side. I just wonder if he felt the same for all the Poll

Tax, May Day and Wapping rioters, their families and the areas they affected?

'They do not work so that these mindless idiots can ruin their lives because their team can't score a goal.' And people don't stand outside a ground to be attacked by riot police as they are eating a bag of chips. What are you going to do? He also said that the hooligans could not class themselves as football fans. 'They just wanted to prove that they were tougher than other people.' Which is exactly why you attacked us. And no, we wanted to prove to the Old Bill that they were not going to intimidate us. As far as we were concerned that night, we were never going to get at Birmingham. The police had them completely cordoned off. We were just milling about with no great expectation of anything happening. Then the police charged; different ball game now. Without that charge, the whole night would never have happened.

The Metropolitan Police threatened to sue Millwall after the events. It was only after our club chairman, Theo Paphitis, donated money to the injured officers' charity and introduced the controversial ID card scheme did they back down.

How could Millwall be held responsible? It was about half-a-mile from the ground. How far exactly from the ground and how long after a game is Millwall, or any football club, to be held responsible for the followers of that club? Inside the ground and during the game, the club is culpable. West Ham are aware of that fact. 'There was no fighting in the ground.' Great. Half-a-mile away and ten minutes after the final whistle? Morally responsible? Five miles away and two hours after the game finished? Not sure that will stand up in court. Where exactly does the club's responsibility end? It is this grey area that allows all the 'relevant authorities' to throw this back and forth to each other. Even now the Government blames clubs, clubs blame police, who blame the Government, who blame clubs, who blame ... suffice to say, the threat of suing Millwall by the Met Police was at best a frivolous notion. Some may call that extortion. Though not me, of course.

Theo Paphitis said after the events, 'Where incidents occur away from The Den, we do, of course, feel a moral responsibility.' I think Theo knew he was on safe ground. 'But the problem of mob violence is not solely a Millwall problem, it is not a football problem, it is a problem which plagues the whole of society.' Over to you, Met Police and Government, is exactly what Theo appears to be saying there.

After the night, three men were charged with public order offences. Another was charged with a breach of a banning order. On top of that two others were arrested outside the ground and warned for drunkenness. Another was released with no further action. Hardly the outbreak of World War III. You get more arrested in a punch-up at a family do in The Dog & Duck at Grandma's 80th birthday. Although Chief Superintendent Mike Humphrey said, 'This is my seventh season as Commander for Millwall and this is the worst yet.' It lasted for over an hour after being charged by the police. We threw bricks, stones, a chisel, flares and fireworks at them. Two cars were set alight. Someone from Scotland Yard said, out of 36 mounted police officers, 24 were injured and so were 24 horses. She said one whole 21-strong unit of riot police was wounded. Nine of the injured were treated in hospital for injuries including a broken arm, leg and foot. Sure, the injuries the police inflicted at the May Day and Poll Tax riots vastly outnumbered these.

Millwall president Reg Burr said that all troublemakers would get a lifetime ban. 'We will do anything we can to identify any troublemakers and the appropriate action will be taken –

we will ban them for life.' Naturally, the police warned they had video footage of the disturbances and expected to make a significant number of arrests. They said some of the violence must have been premeditated as weapons had been stashed away ahead of the match.

For the record, the fireworks were for the Birmingham fans – not the police, not their horses, not their dogs. But, after they instigated the trouble with their baton charge, well, people will use anything they can get their hands on to fight back.

Three years later, we drew Birmingham in the Carling Cup at The Den. They brought 1,500 fans, including a firm of about 300 hooligans. They did not do anything.

35

TALKING OF
MILLWALL ...

George Graham:
'The Millwall fans reminded me of home. The ground may have
been a bit spartan, but I soon realised that the fans were in a
different class. In fact, their passion for the game reminded me
of my days in Glasgow. The people up there are really fanatical
about their football, they eat it and sleep it, and the Millwall
fans were exactly the same. That was something I wasn't used
to, because I thought that, in general, Southerners were less
passionate. I learned so much.'

Reg Burr, former chairman of the club:
'Millwall are a convenient coat peg for football to hang its social
ills on.'

Marc Ceeste, Professor at Hoegaarden University and Millwall
fan:
'Violence has always been an undercurrent at the club. It is part
of the fabric of Millwall life and to deny it is foolishness.'

Peter Simpson, 35, Southend, Essex:

'It was kicking off all over the place and the police didn't seem to be able to stop it ... there was quite a few injured.'

Skip, Everton:
'I was in the boy's pen section of the Gwladys Street Stand the day Millwall came to town. A half-full tin of Party Seven bitter was thrown from the Upper Gwladys Street on to a group of away fans who had bungled their way into the Gwladys Street. This sparked a charge from Millwall causing a hand-to-hand scrap of fists, bottles and sticks. It all felt so bizarre as New Seekers rang out from the Tannoy with the words, "*I'd like to teach the world to sing ...*" Fucking scary they were.

Ben Newton, West Ham fan from Harrow in London:
'My father had been stretchered away after being hit with a dart in the head.'

Millwall fan:
'Millwall have been in the top league of violence but bottom leagues at football. When you sign up to follow Millwall, glory is the last thing on your mind.'

QPR fan:
'I personally had to slide out of the Men's in the stands when two Millwall hooligans raced in with knives. Didn't stay around long enough to find out what happened.'

Brighton Boy:
'We played Millwall and beat them 2–1. Players started fighting on the pitch. A Millwall fan ran on the pitch and drop-kicked our Brighton player Mark Beeney. Fucking mad.'

Fergal O'Brien:
'I saw a West Ham fan getting punched in the face by a burly, bald man who had a coin between his fist.'

Theo Paphitis:
'Once again, the thuggish element which sees football as a cover for their violent tendencies has sullied the name of football and Millwall, and brought deep distress to our local community with whom we have close ties. We also wish to express our sympathy to those police officers and horses injured. We have worked tirelessly over the past several years to rid ourselves of the mindless minority.'

Anon:
'Millwall are not alone in harbouring a hooligan minority, but it is the unrepentant nature of the mob that demands attention and contempt.'

SE4 JW:
'No one likes the Millwall thugs – and the Millwall thugs do not care.'

Mick Wall:
'Millwall are seen outside London as the underdogs to the capital's Premiership giants, the put-upon poor relations tucked away in a working-class corner in the south-east of the city.
It is now almost ingrained in the culture of the mob that they can at least cling to their superiority as hooligans to challenge their more illustrious neighbours.'

Chief Executive Andy Ambler:
'We've come a long way in the last 20 years when it was almost commonplace at every game.'

Football League spokesman Ian Christon:
'There were disgraceful scenes and nobody wants to see that connected with football. We hope the police press charges against the Millwall fans involved and the courts take action to ban these people from football grounds.'

Millwall fan:
'We took 3,000 up to Maine Road after they threatened us with loads of stuff about what they were going to do after that night at The Den. To avoid getting an escort, about 500 'Wall got off at Stockport and were milling by that pub near the station. I remember the roundabout coming to a complete standstill and a few lairy Stockport lads getting slapped. Man United came down, too, en route to somewhere and 'Wall chased them back down the hill. It was quite a sight for sleepy old Stockport ... and that landlord said it was the best day's takings he'd ever had and thanked us all and promised he'd go to the Caribbean or some such on it! Millwall then went on their way to Moss Side and marched through without a peep from City fans. Pathetic Mancs. The next time we had Man City, they banned us for some strange reason!'

Wall One:
'Our behaviour at the 2004 FA Cup Final was exemplary, with the Cardiff police reporting no arrests of any of the Millwall supporters.'

Anon:
'Harsher Prison sentences because some of them should never be allowed to walk the streets again. And public birching. The current community service punishment is pathetic.'

Michael Hart of the *Evening Standard*:
'The club has been successful in combating the hooligan image that has hounded them for nearly two decades. They are unkempt, unfashionable and unloved but are making strident efforts on and off the field to present a more acceptable face to the public.'

Cardiff fan:
'All of a sudden, we were surrounded by the biggest geezers I had ever seen. They were right in our faces shouting, "Is this a joke? Where's your big boys?" I was absolutely terrified. We shuffled along and these psychos were all around us, and every now and again they would smack one of us. They were just taking the piss out of us and there was nothing we could do. Dai Ellis jumps out and says: "I'm not having this, let's do them." Smack – he's rolling down the bank getting kicked stupid. The whole thing goes mental and we are trying to fight back but it's useless.'

West Ham fan:
'I was walking up and a group of hooligans came for us … the police wanted to help but they were clearly afraid to use force … I am still shaking, I thought I was going to die.'

Birmingham fan:
'Our 13 coaches take off and I'm falling asleep against the window as we've been driving through London for about 15

minutes. All of a sudden the windows on the coach are caving in and we are surrounded by hundreds of Millwall. We're lying on the floor as more and more bricks hit the coach. Noddy opens the exit and says, "Let's do 'em." Balls to that, man, there were millions of them.'

Forest:
'In the ground, Millwall were in the next enclosure. Panda pop glass bottles were raining down on us, darts were flying through the air and a black pool ball was thrown back and forth all through the game. Millwall were singing "*We are evil ...*" over and over and I was having kittens. The final whistle goes and they let Millwall out and keep us in for 20 minutes. "Here we go," I think, "we're dead for sure now."'

F-Troop:
'I am not going for some dirty northern ponce to spit all over me ... if he spits over me, I'll put a fucking pint glass in his head. People are scared of us all over England.'

36

SPORTING GENIUS...
AND STUPIDITY

Sport was the brainchild of the ruling classes from the late nineteenth century. Don't get me wrong now – sport was nothing new. All the Victorian ruling classes must have done was have a conversation along the lines of: 'I say, ye olde plebs becometh a tad unruly in my constituency, Lord Wilbersten-Force. What sayeth you?'

'Same, same, old bean ... just wondering ... how did ye olde Greeks and Caesar control the masses? Did they give them some sort of outlet?'

'Indeed, once a week they had them fighting each other and the lions in the gladiators' ring and, of course, the Greeks invented the Olympics.'

'Sport ... that's it ... sport! Church, Sunday ... sport, Saturday ... '

'Excellent, My Lord.'

'Thank you, My Lord.'

'Another brandy?'

'Marvellous, isn't it ... '

There has always been the need for an outlet for the high spirits of the working classes. This was recognised by the élite old boys who created the FA in 1863. And it's still run by the élite today. No longer was religion enough of an opiate; we needed something new. Sitting in the pews kept us quiet, unquestioning and subservient but they recognised we needed something more. Even the loudest chorus of 'Jerusalem' wouldn't quench or satisfy the need to scream and shout of the average man working and toiling all week. That need to let off steam. A release valve.

Sunday was sorted – Church and fear – so they needed something to distract us plebs on a Saturday. A new church with a new fear. Thus were the seeds for *Kick Off*, *Match of the Day*, *Grandstand* and, ultimately, Sky Sports sewn. Solely for the hooligan in you and the hooligan in all of us. Put simply, if the working classes became obsessed by sport and their activities of a Saturday and Sunday, they wouldn't be thinking of overthrowing the government or the ruling classes every two minutes. Hence modern-day sport was born.

Football is one of the children of sport. It became the favourite son for many. Then it evolved into the favourite child of the nation – from the first club that was formed in Sheffield to the biggest sport on planet earth. That first club had no opposition; they were the only club around at the time. Imagine forming a one-man chess league. Lunatics? Oh no, not only were they revolutionaries but they were ingenious, too. They used to play bachelors versus husbands, over 25s versus under 25s, brown hair versus all the rest, pit workers versus steel workers – whatever. Not sure of the last few match-ups but they used to make teams. The first league was formed a few years later, including Accrington Stanley. The purpose? To give the working classes an outlet for all that extra testosterone that Victorian society would not allow them to release anywhere, let alone in the bedroom.

It was something devised, provided, allowed and encouraged solely as an outlet for the virile young men of that era without threatening the social hierarchy. When it kicked off as expected, with thousands of drunken proles fighting, then the directors would be looking down mockingly: 'My boys are off again ... I banned overtime on the docks this week, guffaw, guffaw.' Dockers traditionally are hard-working, hard-drinking, hard-fighting hard men, and Millwall has dockers tattooed on its soul.

So naturally we buy into it at Millwall. Release all that pent-up frustration and testosterone. And a few years down the line the same ruling classes call us mindless morons! And through the power of the press that they control, they convince the world that the concept they started – letting off steam for the plebs at the match – is now borderline World War III.

Well, here's what I say – 'Fuck off!' I know where it was all born from. We are now the cast aside and castigated children of the ruling classes' concept. It's like they gave us a little cub to play with to keep us quiet, turned their backs and it's turned into a roaring lion they have no control over.

Football hooliganism has only attracted widespread media attention and disdain in the last 40 years or so, yet its roots go as far back as the very early days of the game in the late 1800s. Gangs of supporters would intimidate neighbourhoods and attack opposing supporters, players and referees. Letting off steam was the whole intention. Hooliganism as it is currently recognised in England has its roots in the Sixties, when the Government created the Public Order Act 1968. It allowed the Courts to ban offenders from football grounds. More legislation followed with the Taylor Report and the Football Disorder Act. The definition of 'hooligan' had broadened widely and, over a few short years, the ruling class had achieved their objectives through legislation. They had changed society's perceptions and sent to Coventry the word 'hooligan' and all who sailed in her.

It is not the actions of fans that has changed; that has always been the same. What has changed is society's perception of those actions. Perception is controlled by the mass media; the mass media is controlled by the ruling classes; the ruling class control the masses, how we think and what we think about. If they want to change our perception of something, they do so. What we accept today they can make us frown at on tomorrow. They simply pass some new legislation, which they did, and what was acceptable yesterday is frowned upon today.

After the World Cup Final in 1966 no one mentioned the pitch invasion. Technically, Germany could have claimed what Forest did in 1974 after losing at Newcastle, 'We were intimidated by the crowd.' The nation did not notice because it was 1966, acceptable, and England playing. But roll the clock forward 20 years and they have changed our perception.

Remember now the Eighties and when it was a club side playing. Oh, what a different story, but it is still just some people on the pitch pretending it is all over. And when that club side was Millwall? Oh, what a different story times ten. Or are we all paranoid at Millwall?

The question is not how they changed our perspective. That is clear. They control the legislative process and the press, so they control us. Like putty in their hands, we are. No, the real question is: Why? Why, after devising, providing, allowing and encouraging this 'letting off steam' from 1880–1968 did they decide to move the goalposts? For almost 90 years, they did not give a toss. Looked down like Caesars laughing at their playthings. Did they just wake up bored and decide to have a 'head-fuck the plebs day'? Because I can definitely believe that. Bored as fuck and wanted to mess with our minds. It could have been for financial gain, always a primary motive in all their actions. Plebs had televisions now, gates were at an all-time low, homes were more homely than ever and it could have been to draw more people back to the game. Maybe they just didn't see us as the threat they once did and didn't feel the need to allow us to let off steam anymore. Or had we become too much of a threat, with a potential revolution once again a fear?

Whatever, they decided to ban a good old punch-up at the match. But as we know, for every action there is an equal and opposite reaction and maybe that explains the apparent 'explosion' of football hooliganism in the Seventies and Eighties. We are only human. Tell us we can't do something and we will go out and do it all the more. The peasants revolted; we are plebs to the ruling classes but we still had a bit of rebel spunk in us then.

Obviously, they highlight Millwall in the press and we are the perennial scapegoats. It's time to see that as a compliment now. It is only because our firm is so good that we are in the news. Little firms getting a hiding every week are not going to make front-page, national news. Only the winners make the headlines. We all know that. We are victims of our own success. That is the way to think of it.

Question: If our firm was being pummelled week in and week out, would we be the story we are today?

No fucking chance!

37

FRIDAY NIGHT, BRISTOL'S ALL RIGHT

They had changed our away match against Bristol City in March 2001 to a Friday night game to keep down the travelling numbers. We still took nearly 1,200 fans in an attendance of just over 10,000. I have always liked the idea of these games because your weekends start early. We had an early meet in The Gregorian on Jamaica Road. I got there about 12.00pm and, by 2.00pm, it was filling up. About 20 of us decided to go up to Central London to carry on drinking. We made our way from Bermondsey Tube station to Covent Garden, then headed to The Punch & Judy, a good pub in the pedestrian area.

After a couple of hours we went to Paddington to catch the train. We knew we would get a lively reception in Bristol. We were met by the usual over-the-top police escort at Temple Meads and marched all the way to Ashton Gate. People were getting annoyed. Little arguments and scuffles were breaking out with the Old Bill all along the way. It took ages and, by the time we had reached the ground, the match had started. As we approached the turnstiles, it started to kick off with the Old Bill again. Then we heard Bristol City had scored. This did not help the situation. Now we were even more determined to get into the ground.

We ran for the turnstiles and, once inside, we ran a gauntlet of missiles from the home fans through a tunnel between the home and away sections. We stopped halfway and started returning the objects that had come our way. As more Millwall were coming behind us, it was hard to hold our position and we were pushed into the away end. We had missed the first 15 minutes. The Old Bill and stewards had completely boxed us in.

It was a rip-snorting atmosphere because we were making plenty of noise and singing as loud as the home fans, who were giving it loads behind the safety of the Old Bill. Then we got a pen and Harris scored. We went fucking mental. A fair few objects came our way – the usual coins and lighters.

In the second half, the referee sent off our two strikers, Moody and Harris, and then he played eight minutes' injury time. Just to top it off, he awarded them a penalty – 2–1. And people wonder why we are so paranoid about conspiracy theories! At the final whistle, we attempted to get at the Bristol fans. The Old Bill stood firm. With batons raised and ready, they were cracking people over the head and pushing us back. And the home fans, too. Then from behind they came under a barrage of missiles from Bristol, mainly seats and coins. There was a stand-off between all three mobs before the police forced us outside. They just wanted rid now and to get us to the station in the shortest time possible.

Bristol were mobbing behind the police. A few Millwall broke the police lines and attacked the home fans and had the better of the exchanges. On the way back to the station, some more Bristol appeared. Again the police line was broken but they ran away when we got through.

On the way up on the train, we had discussed staying in

Bristol for the night so getting out of the escort was essential for us. Me and three of the chaps got near the front and veered off to the right. Although sticking together, we were now easy targets to be picked off, but with these other three and me, we were a match for anyone. From previous visits we knew Bristol quite well and headed for a hotel that we had stayed in before. We ended up partying the night away, bouncing round the city with no trouble at all and jumped the train back to London on the Saturday morning. Friday night games work.

38

HOOLIGANISM – PURE GENIUS

It is any wonder problems have persisted when one of our initiatives to tackle hooliganism in 1982/83 went like this: the club wanted to introduce ID cards, to include your name and two photos. The ground was to be divided into three sections – away fans, card holders and non-card holders. Here's where the fun starts. If a fan was caught causing trouble, the only section they would be allowed to enter would be … the away end. The theory or thinking behind it? Hopefully, they would be in the minority. Genius. Truly fucking genius. The end for our away fans would have been packed full every home game with our biggest hooligans, lunatics, headcases and nutters. Who or what the fuck were these people in the corridors of power thinking?

'We caught 200 hooligans last week, Mr Chairman. Not one had an ID card.'

'Oh, right you are, throw them all in the away end for the next home game.'

'Good shout, Mr Chairman. That should put a stop to the trouble.'

Fan-fucking-tastic, we would have thought! No police

cordon to break, just straight into their end, wait for 'Mmmmiiillwaaalll' to go up and let the fun begin. Honestly, where the fuck do they get some of their ideas from?

That 'initiative' did not get off the ground. Cannot think why myself, although the club has tried to address the problem. Sort of. Really not sure if they were trying to eliminate the problem or just paying a bit of lip service to it. The Football Community scheme was one of the first initiatives launched at many clubs in the Seventies as a counter-measure to hooliganism. The club was aiming to involve young people in a variety of football-related activities and help build strong links between the club and community, in the hope that these kids would not go on to be future hooligans by keeping them off the streets and in coaching courses and educational projects.

All football clubs have introduced a number of measures to reduce trouble. The change to all-seater stadiums and the introduction of family enclosures were recommendations following The Taylor Report. The introduction of CCTV and increased stewarding, as well as the use of banning orders, are all now utilised in tackling the problem. There is also greater co-operation between clubs, police and the media in helping to find and prosecute hooligans. Technology is a tool for them.

The Government's Working Group on Football Related Disorder also published a number of recommendations to tackle football hooliganism. It wants to see a bigger role for fans that are keen to tackle violence as well as greater recognition by clubs of the role of fans. Typical Government plan, really. In effect, they want everyone to grass on their next-door neighbours and want the clubs to endorse it. It also wants to see clubs control the sales of tickets for away games where trouble is likely to occur. Of course it does; the Government is trying to address the problem by getting the clubs to solve it, because it doesn't know what the fuck to do itself.

They are using the television now, too. On 28 October 2009, the West Ham v Millwall game popped up on *Crimewatch*. A DCI Tucker was telling us to grass up 66 geezers on a website. A nation of grassers is exactly what they want.

39

SEASONAL MADNESS

There were about 14 press-reported incidents during the 2001/02 season. It seemed we were in the papers almost every week and most of the incidents were no worse than previous events that had received no coverage in the local or national papers. Suddenly someone sneezes and it produces a full-page spread. Was it coincidence that the BBC were simultaneously running an undercover operation?

This drip-feeding to the public of their Millwall hooligan fix began in August and culminated in May – precisely when the documentary was shown on BBC2. If that was a coincidence then the BBC documentary film-makers probably could not believe their luck. 'Millwall are off again.'

So what happened during the Mad Season?

No doubt we caught the Old Bill on the hop when we played Spurs at home in August 2001. At 11.00am, more than 100 of our finest travelled to an arranged meeting with the Tottenham Yid Army on Jamaica Road in Bermondsey. Spurs took a kicking after some vicious fighting before police reinforcements split the two groups. The Old Bill and Spurs fans again came under heavy and sustained attack from us near the ground. Both firms left the match ten minutes before the final whistle to continue our battle. About 30 police officers and three police horses were injured during the day. One man was also taken to hospital with knife wounds. A good hiding for Spurs on the day.

Then at the end of the month, we had Birmingham away. It was a Sunday and an early kick-off so we arranged to meet at Euston Station at about 10.00am. A good turnout. We took a few thousand fans that day, and most of them would have been ready for a tear-up. Thirty or so of our normal lot. Loads of Old Bill on the platform and on the train; loads more at Birmingham. Modern football journeys mean being surrounded by police. So first it was the Met, then we were passed on to the British Transport Police, I guess, and then passed on again to the Midlands' finest. A big operation between the three forces, plus the spotters and minglers – those who pretend to be Millwall fans undercover, essentially intelligence officers travelling with us to see who they can pick out. The 'known troublemakers'. Some task they have on their hands, with a couple of thousand of us mooching up to Brum.

Sometimes, some of our boys have a crack with the Old Bill. Me – never. I steer clear of them as much as possible. My face is known well enough already without having any banter with them. To me, they're always the enemy. Why do some of our boys have a laugh with them? I guess some just like to take the piss. Others, maybe ones that had no intention of fighting at the game, probably felt safe enough to have banter. A speccy, wonky little cop has always been fair game, or a tidy little bird cop. She's always at the end of a bit of Millwall mouth. Basically, the boys would push it as far as they felt they could.

The Old Bill could always turn round and nick you at any given time. The wise ones realise that trying to nick a Millwall fan on the train that is rammed with Millwall fans is not a good idea. I can't remember too many of our boys getting nicked on a train like that. So maybe the cops are not that stupid. They more than likely earmark the real mouthy boys – a quiet nicking by picking off a straggler at the back is a lot easier than on the train.

On days like this, they have their hands full all day. Two hours of abuse from boarding to getting off. Part of the fun of the day is listening to the Old Bill getting grief. Passes the time. These are all officially dry trains but, of course, there are ways around this. One of our favourites is a bottle of Coke or lemonade – take a couple of glasses out and fill it to the brim with vodka. It stays the same colour. It keeps us happy. It keeps us occupied on the train. Probably about five or six carriages and the train was packed.

After getting there, we were held at New Street station for a while, waiting for the next train so they could take us all together. Trying to control us and keep us together is their main objective at this stage. Two mobs of 1,000 strong are much harder to control than one mob of 2,000.

Nothing had been arranged with the Zulus but we were hopeful of breaking the police cordon. Fair play, we were surrounded by Old Bill on the journey to the ground – hundreds of police, riot vans, dogs, the usual police presence that followed us everywhere. So I wasn't expecting the Zulus to be there before us. Hoping, yes, not expecting, though.

We got in the ground with still not a Zulu in sight. I remember during the game three black spotters come down and had a good look at us. It was Cuddles and two of his sidekicks. A few wolf-whistles and they soon walked away. I suppose they look harder in the eyes of the rest of their firm. All this bullshit and bravado from these three still makes me laugh, though. Nothing happened at all during the game, other than we were 4-0 down at half time. Gutted.

The game finished and we were herded back to the station. Birmingham tried to attack us, and we are aware that stuff was going on, but they were never in danger of getting to us and we were never going to be able to break the police cordon. It was probably about four deep of riot Old Bill, all with their full gear on and their dogs. Never could count how many dogs. Plus mounted Old Bill with truncheons, vans and cars. There was a helicopter overhead as well, I am sure. Dogs barking, people shouting, chaos it was. Chaos.

It was about this time that tactical riot gear came in and the police got more organised. This wasn't like the old Keystone cop days as a couple of Old Bill ran around with their helmets falling off while two firms kicked fuck out of each other. These were massive, sophisticated police operations; it was virtually impossible to break out of these cordons. Then Wolves turned up. We already knew they were going to turn up because we were being held up to let them go before us. Pretty efficiently done, really. They kept us outside for about half-an-hour while they shunted a few trains with fans they did not want us to meet. Nothing like Rorke's Drift was going on with the Zulus outside. I think they made one little, half-hearted effort just to say that they'd had a go but the Old Bill were well on top of them.

Still, they tried, eh? The Old Bill had started to get organised. They had taken their time. Over 30 years to realise the fundamentals of crowd control but, by this stage, having turned to Robocop lookalikes, the three forces combined on a day like that probably outnumbered us. The turn of the 21st century had most definitely seen a change in the way it was now being handled by the Old Bill. A pretty fucking bad day all round. Got dicked by Brum and got wrapped up from start to finish by Old Bill. Couldn't wait to get back to Euston to get a drink and ended up in The Globe on Baker Street. Eight or nine hours of being totally wrapped up by the police on a day like that. You actually do not feel as if you are out of their grasp until you put your head on your pillow. All in all, pretty uneventful but a sign that maybe, for this new season and from here onwards, being a Millwall fan travelling away was going to be harder.

Just a couple of days later we had Cardiff at home and we were hoping for better. It was another of those potentially explosive, mid-week fixtures in the first round of the Worthington Cup. Again, though, we had the Kings of Wales which meant a no-show from Cardiff. Bit of a surprise? Not really. After we had taken the piss a couple of years earlier and they failed to show up, I don't think anyone was shocked to see another no-show from this lot.

After the game, some young Millwall fans had a bit of fun with the police and they ran riot in the streets around the ground. Cars and shops were smashed and bricks and bottles were thrown at the Old Bill long into the night. Press reports certainly over-exaggerated the events. I'd never get too involved with that; that wasn't the idea of it for me. Maybe that is a bit of a change due to the policing methods. They tie up the fans and the younger ones, deprived of an opportunity of facing any away fans, then turn their attentions to the Old Bill. Me, I was in the pub having a right good old drink. A couple of fellas came in and mentioned it was kicking off with the police but we just stayed in and got pissed. Had to get up and work the next day. Plus, of course, I steer clear of Old Bill as much as possible.

Just four days after the Cardiff game, there was a repeat performance as the young Millwall fans attacked the police because they were pissed off at not getting to Burnley. Once they start, the kids do not care; they will fight with the Old Bill and go on the rampage. It is all part of their day out. One Old Bill in an interview said, 'We've tried everything, keeping away fans in late, keeping the home fans in late, letting away fans go, letting them go early ... and nothing works.' I could have told him that. It is a melting pot that sometimes boils over. Twice in four days it simmered and bubbled at the end of summer, then, after a good drink up, the younger fans took the piss out of the Old Bill.

After the events of 9/11, the press were diverted for a while. They had new, international, jet-stealing hooligans to report on now, but they were soon back on their favourite topic – Millwall – and a home match with Forest to get their juices flowing. There was another major police operation to keep us apart, which was a big blow because Forest had come and looked like they were going to have a good firm. Again, it turned out as a fight with the police, who must have been thinking, 'On the one hand, aren't we good stopping all the football hooligans getting at each other? On the other ... we are having more trouble with these Millwall boys than if we just let the two sets of fans crack on at each other ...'

And while the Old Bill must have been severely pissed off at all the aggro coming their way, we were sick and tired of being wrapped up by them. So what did we do? Well, in October, for Wolves away, we became the early birds again. A group of about 200 of us were there and a load of us burst through the police lines at Wolverhampton station. We attacked a pub near Molineux where members of their firm were drinking. Wolves took a mini-hiding and dashed in the pub, not before a couple were slashed in the face. Police split us up, saving the rest of the Subway Army. Unfortunately, it was not as big a ruck as we had hoped for and, after the one attack, our early arrival was scuppered. The Old Bill soon had us wrapped up, but any press story that highlights police incompetence is newsworthy. It was heavily reported anyway.

And in December, for Portsmouth at home, we had been in touch with their firm by mobile. A meet was arranged well away from the Old Bill with Portsmouth in The Windmill near Waterloo Station. We arrived and attacked the pub with bottles, bricks and dustbin lids. Portsmouth responded by throwing everything back. Every window of the pub was smashed while most of the furniture in the pub was either broken or ended up outside. After the match, Portsmouth had another little go, coming off the worst again and a few of them took a good kicking outside the ground. It was a decent effort by a game little Pompey firm, nothing major, really, and hardly a return to the battlegrounds of old. Heavily reported.

In January 2002, we had Birmingham at home, where a half-eaten pie was thrown at a linesman by a Millwall fan. You would have thought all the officials had been hung, drawn and quartered with the press coverage on this one. Let us keep a bit of perspective please ... it was a fucking pie.

There were more headlines later in January when we played Blackburn at home, because a car clamper van targeted a line of Millwall supporters' cars after being employed by a private local estate. When the fans returned to their vehicles, the mood turned ugly and the police were called. The clamper's own van was overturned and the fans' cars were released without fines being imposed. Police describe the clamper as either the 'bravest or most stupid man alive'. Ten out of ten for all those involved.

Yet another 'unprecedented security operation' was put in place in February for Forest away, to prevent us from clashing in Nottingham. An extra 270 police officers were deployed, 36 pubs were closed and the kick-off was moved to noon in a successful bid to stop any trouble. Apparently, about half of the Forest firm were spotted drinking before kick-off. They boarded a train due to arrive in Nottingham at the same time as a train 'full of known Millwall hooligans'. Police held our train back. After the game, there was a stand-off between Forest and the police while we were escorted to the train station. So where was the story? Police were at the match? Struggling now with only weeks until the documentary is aired. This was heavily reported.

In March, we headed to Portsmouth for an early game as kick-off was brought forward to noon in a bid to prevent trouble from breaking out. Before and after the match, we tried to get at each other but were kept apart by a wall of police wearing riot helmets and wielding batons. We taunted each other and threw missiles along the way but absolutely fuck all happened. So press reports hammered home that roads were closed to traffic and pubs were shut. Shocking.

Again in March, we attacked Sheffield Wednesday as they left the ground after a home game. Old Bill stopped us and a couple of officers were hit with bricks and bottles and two needed hospital treatment. Outbreak of scandalous proportions, eh?

Then for Wolves at home in April, we were hopeful a big firm would come up to seek revenge. They arrived in Paddington but were spotted by two police officers. Their coach was escorted to The Den. Press reports stated: 'A huge policing operation (more than 300 officers) prevented the hooligan groups from clashing.' That was true. So we pelted Old Bill with bricks, bottles and fireworks as we attempted to get to the Wolves firm. Big fucking deal. Nothing had happened but the stories just kept on coming.

Was this a mad season or not? One good ruck against Spurs in a pre-season game and the early away trip to Wolves. Fuck all major, really. BBC documentary makers must have been getting a bit twitchy. They were still reading press reports but must have been desperate for something big to happen, something catastrophic ... something like a riot. Only speaking hypothetically, of course, but that hypothetical wish came true after an unprecedented baton charge straight at us by the riot police that made no sense at all.

And then their luck changed in May: 'A total of 45 police officers were injured when trouble erupted after Millwall lost to Birmingham in the Division One play-offs.' A group of about 900 of us spent an hour throwing missiles including bricks, paving stones, a chisel, flares and fireworks at the Old Bill. Two cars were also set alight. Nine officers required hospital treatment. A number of police horses were also injured, two seriously. A total of seven people were arrested. The night fizzled out and so came the end of the mad season.

The maddest thing for me about the mad season? The coincidence of all the constant press reports with the culmination of the broadcast on BBC2 – *Undercover with the Hooligans* – perfectly in sync with an unprecedented baton charged instigated by a police riot. Mad.

40

STRANGERS IN OUR MIDST

West Ham, Chelsea, Leeds, Man City and others have all had successful operations to infiltrate them. Undercover police have taken out the leaders and made arrests that brought the firm down. The police on numerous occasions have not been able to get inside our firm. With there being no real hierarchy and no leader or figurehead since Harry the Dog, it makes it very difficult for the Old Bill. Arrests have been made but they didn't affect the week-in, week-out continuation of the firm.

An early attempt was Operation Full Time Millwall Bushwackers, a five-month surveillance and infiltration operation in 1987 that ended with seven arrests. In Court, they were charged with conspiracy. The prosecution offered no evidence. Five months, with how many Old Bill on overtime? And for what? Nothing! And to stop what? A punch-up. Is it really worth it? Open up the park, throw 500 of us and 500 ICF in and let's get it on. Cost to police? Nothing. They could even charge a fiver to the spectators.

Undeterred by their failure to pin a case on someone, they gave it another shot. Obviously one of their bright sparks had been impressed by Leslie Grantham and *EastEnders* because the next undercover effort was called Operation Dirty Den. Fucking genius again. You can't knock their 'Name the Operation' department. Always simple – but effective. Well done to them. Operation Dirty Den was a minor success – 16 arrests were made in dawn raids and six men were put in front of the judge on 27 January 1988. The men were charged with fighting and affray. The trial lasted six months and two men were convicted – Keith Wilcox, 27, and Simon Taylor, 20. It was a jury decision of 11–1. On hearing the verdict, the one juror stood up and said, 'Scapegoats, bloody scapegoats … it's bloody true, that's what they were.' Taylor received three years, Wilcox four and the juror seven days. On 24 January 1989 at the Royal Courts of Justice, Lord Chief Justice of England (Lord Lane) and two appeal judges found in favour of acquittal on appeal through lack of evidence.

In April 1988, two more fans were arrested and accused of 'Havoc and Mayhem' at a football match. Fuelled by this unmitigated success, the police had another go and, in February 1990, six Millwall fans were arrested for singing and gesticulating at a match. Yes, you heard correctly – singing and gesticulating at a football match. What scandal!

Outsiders were even more frowned upon following these operations. Everyone knows each other in their own firm so that made it extremely hard for the police to infiltrate successfully in an undercover operation. Consequently, it proved very difficult for the police to arrest, caution, prosecute and convict. They eventually realised this and started to use other methods. Nowadays they use spotters, video evidence and the press print mug shots and photos to help arrest people after events. They also now CCTV you in a ruck, identify and then arrest you in early morning raids.

They arrested a further 16 across London and Hertfordshire

one morning. A new day had indeed dawned. All had been identified from CCTV footage taken after disturbances at our home matches against Wolves on 21 January and against Palace on 18 February. The swoop followed the arrest of ten men a couple of months earlier who were charged with violent disorder. Old Bill sought banning orders against the men to stop them from entering all Premiership, League and Conference football grounds. All of the arrests were part of Operation Devine, the Met's newest crackdown on home and away supporters acting violently at Millwall matches.

A Superintendent BJ Harrington, who led Operation Devine, was quoted as saying, 'Those identified and arrested as part of today's pre-planned operation have used the veneer of football to legitimise senseless violence. We recognise that the majority of football fans just want to enjoy the game and, as such, we know that they, and the football clubs involved, support all police activity in removing violent disorder from in and around the grounds.' We want to enjoy the game, too. Just let us have our little ruck in the park first.

'We will work closely with the courts to ensure that banning orders are imposed, which, in turn, will prevent them from causing any further trouble at future matches.'

Nice one, BJ – but I've got a bit of bad news for you on that front. Millwall FC chief executive Ken Brown said, 'The success of Operation Devine is good news for football fans and good news for Millwall Football Club.' Fair play, Ken. You would not expect him to come out and say, 'Bollocks, that is ten less through the turnstiles next week.' Partly, of course, because he also knows banning orders do not work. 'It sends out a clear message that the minority who seek to use football matches as an excuse to exhibit violent behaviour will be prosecuted. We operate a zero-tolerance policy in respect of such behaviour at

Millwall and fully support the police in their initiative.' Of course you do, Ken. What a lad. Behind you all the way.

'The vast majority of decent, law-abiding fans who watch matches at The Den can be reassured they will continue to be able to watch football in a safe environment.' Of course it is safe, Ken. Our firm ensures that. If we were not there, all the other firms would come down to The Den and completely run riot, a'raping and a'pillaging and doing what the fuck they please on our manor. The vast majority of decent, law-abiding fans who watch matches at The Den know they are watching football in the safest environment in the country – because of The Bushwackers. Not fucking despite us.

I think Ken knew that, really, but again, could we truly expect a chief exec to give it the large? 'Our hooligans are the best out there. I go to every home game knowing that no firm in the land is coming to The Den and gonna rip apart our stadium.'

41

SWEET FA

The last time we had reached a semi-final was 1937, so not too many of the chaps were thinking 'Abide with Me' when we met up before this third-round game in January 2004 at The Ancient Foresters in Bermondsey. We weren't expecting any trouble that day either, not against Walsall. There were about 20 of us having a good piss-up before the game. We won 2–1 on an average Saturday. A good win.

There was the usual hysteria surrounding our fourth-round away tie, with Telford spending a fortune on policing, helicopters and loads of Old Bill. Good racket, the Old Bill have got. I mean, these sorts of games have always had the potential for us to go on the rampage but every game has that and Telford's hooligan element was hardly anything to worry about. The first fixture was postponed because of a waterlogged pitch and the re-arranged fixture was cancelled a couple of hours before kick-off. We had arrived at Euston station to be told by other Millwall fans that the game was off. We were already out for the day so a little thing like a cancelled match wasn't going to stop us. We got on the phone and found out that a few others had stopped off in central London when they had heard there was no match. It turned into an all-day session with 30 of us on a pub crawl round Covent Garden.

Eventually, we got to Telford's Buck's Head Ground in February – third time lucky after two cancellations and a big piss-up in Covent Garden. We made the trip to Telford by train arriving just before kick-off for the midweek night game. The pitch was a right mess with sand all over it. We should have killed them off with loads of chances before Paul Ifill scored just before the interval.

The second half was the same as the first with loads of chances going begging before Dennis Wise sealed the victory just before the final whistle. We left the ground and made our way back to the station for the trip back to London. I was half expecting the local nutters to arrange an ambush, but no such luck.

Then before the fifth-round game against Burnley at home, we had a drink in The Bramcote, then made our way round to the ground and into the West Lower. It was a good Cup tie with plenty of near-the-mark tackles, crowd involvement and intimidation. Burnley had a man sent off. Danny Dichio scored the only goal of the game on 70 minutes. We should have had more goals with the amount of possession and chances we had. Thought all the missed chances were going to come back and haunt us as Burnley nearly snatched an equaliser near the end but we hung on. I went back to The Bramcote a happy man. The quarter-finals of the FA Cup, and we were in it. No trouble on or off the pitch.

People were starting to talk about us going all the way to the final. I was never sure. If we got past Tranmere in the sixth round in March, we could draw Man Utd, Arsenal, Fulham, Portsmouth or Sunderland. Apart from the big two, I fancied us to beat the others if we played to our potential on the day. But being a cynical Millwall supporter for 30 years, I thought it was a nap that we would draw Man Utd or Arsenal in the semis. Whatever the outcome, we were guaranteed a good day out if we got to the next round.

We dominated Tranmere at The Den with their 'keeper, John Achterburg, putting on a one-man show to keep us from scoring. He even saved a Kevin Muscat penalty, forcing a replay at Prenton Park, which was scheduled for about ten days later.

During that time, the semi-final draw was made. We had avoided the Premiership teams and our reward would be Sunderland. Having already taken six points off them that season, the prayer books were out as we arranged our trip up to Merseyside. Beat Tranmere and the FA Cup Final was within touching distance. I was starting to hear faint strains of 'Abide with Me'.

A couple of fellas we knew had arranged a coach. We arrived on the Wirral confident of a victory and any nerves were soon settled with two early goals. Then it was a backs-to-the-wall job with us soaking up the pressure and hanging on. Biting my nails right until the end. After the game, we were going mental. The penny had dropped – we were in the last four and 90 minutes from Wembley.

Our celebrations were cut short when someone said Tranmere were outside. We rushed out of the stand into the street. Nothing. As we moved off towards our coach, a few of the Tranmere boys were outside a pub near the ground; one said while on the phone, 'Millwall are here but they are nothing.' Someone stepped forward and punched him in the side of the head; he dropped his phone and ran. The others scattered into the crowd.

We carried on to the coach where the beer was waiting for us. We had stocked up for the way back. Win or lose, we were having a booze-up. On the way back, we stopped off at two service stations. At each one we emptied off the coach and ransacked them. People were walking out with their jackets full up with whatever they fancied. It happened on many occasions when loads of us piled into shops and just took what we wanted. We have travelled all over with no train tickets, got into grounds with no match tickets and ate and drank what we wanted as our mob moving en masse is hard to stop, never mind question. One of the many perks of going away with the 'Wall.

For the semi-final against Sunderland at Old Trafford, we arranged a hotel in Salford. The majority of us made our way up the day before and that afternoon was spent drinking in the hotel bar. There were Millwall all round Manchester. We were expecting some sort of attack from the Manchester hooligan element, especially after United's humiliation at Stockport, City getting done on the Tube in London and the heavy police presence at Maine Road which prevented us from properly getting at each other. This was an ideal opportunity for them as we were sitting ducks in their city. I know if a team had been playing at our stadium, they would not be able to take over the local area.

During the evening, we went out for a drink in the centre of Manchester. A good night out. By late Saturday morning, everyone had arrived and there were about 30 of us. We were all buzzing, talking about being 90 minutes from the final. We made our way to the ground and joined more Millwall in The Trafford pub. It was a good atmosphere. I was looking forward to the game and confident of a win.

The match was much closer than I thought. It was tight, tense and nervous. Our main man, Tim Cahill, had scored in the 26th minute. At the end, everything changed. It seemed like the whole of Millwall were in Manchester, all going absolutely ballistic. It seemed a bit surreal. We had won a semi-final. We had never reached the final before. Semis in 1903, 1907 and 1937 and, in that last appearance, we became the first team from the old Third Division to reach the last four. Now we were in the final. Utter fucking shock. Millwall were on the way to the FA Cup Final ... without a bit of trouble.

This was it – the Final. The biggest day of our lives was getting beamed around the world and watched by millions of people. South-east London would be empty. It would have been a good night to go out on the pull in the local pubs and clubs because all the men were in Cardiff. I even heard a story about a few blokes whose wives were due to have babies at any minute, but the men were making the trip to Cardiff.

A lot has been said about the amount of fans we took to Cardiff – 20,000 or so. The same as when we took 48,000 to Wembley in the Auto Windscreen Final. I do not look at these people with contempt like some people might. I just think that if you are prepared to go to Carlisle on a cold midweek night, or every home game, you are just more passionate about Millwall than the person that goes to watch a couple of Cup finals. To me, it just shows the massive potential the club has. If we were playing in the Premiership regularly, we would get those people through the turnstiles regularly. Following football is a big financial commitment. I can fully understand that some people do not want to spend their money watching what is shit football the majority of the time. From another angle, I know a few blokes that do not go down The Den anymore because they are sick of facing the heartache of watching Millwall lose.

The build-up to the final was a regular topic and not just in our pubs. Every time you turned the television or the radio on it gave a taste of what it is like supporting a successful football side. We probably had more air time in the build up to the final regarding football matters than in all our history. Another discussion between us was if, where and when The Soul Crew would turn up and would United do something after their two recent poor shows.

The coach we booked left south-east London on Saturday morning to arrive in Cardiff for about lunchtime. The coach journey was full of beer with a good party atmosphere. We arrived in Cardiff and headed for a pub where we had arranged to meet some other Millwall. It was still early so plenty more booze was consumed.

The walk to the ground was fucking mad – a sea of blue and white. Kids with their faces painted, people in big, curly, blue-and-white wigs. All ages were there, from the toddlers to the pensioners. The sun was shining on a glorious day for Millwall FC.

Once we were inside the Millennium Stadium, my arm felt sore from shaking hands with people. I had seen hundreds on the way, some of whom I had not seen for years. Everyone had turned out for the biggest game in our history. The noise we created was deafening, easily drowning out Man United's prawn sandwich munchers who we barely heard singing.

The game whizzed by in a bit of a blur but, from the start, Wise and Wilkins got their tactics wrong. Sit back, try to soak up pressure and hit them on the break. Suicide, especially against a quality team like United. This has never been the Millwall way. We should have been attacking them and putting them under pressure, biting their ankles and trying to force them to make mistakes. What do you expect from Ray Wilkins? Mr Negative. With his game plan, we had one shot on goal in the first half. Ronaldo scored for United just before half time.

The second half was more of the same, with United scoring another two goals. The only good tactical decision Wise and

Wilkins made was to bring Curtis Weston on. He broke Paul Allen's (West Ham) record of the youngest player to appear in the FA Cup Final. The match finished with us still making the same level of noise that had continued from start to finish.

After the game, our supporters stayed to applaud our players and soak up the last bit of atmosphere. We got back to the pub hoping either Cardiff or Manchester would show up. Nothing. We boarded our coach back to London still bouncing. One of the best days of our lives. And the next season would bring about our first European adventure.

42

GUILTY UNTIL PROVEN INNOCENT

I would like to take this opportunity, as someone involved in the Millwall hooligan firm for over 40 years, to apologise unreservedly to anyone reading this book – and, in fact, to the nation as a whole. I cannot and would not deny my responsibility and culpability. You see, on Monday, 28 August 2000, the Government rushed through Parliament the Football Disorder Act. It completely obliterated the civil rights of every man, woman and child in the UK. It was exactly what the Government wanted to do and it was passed under the guise of a Hooligan Bill. It is part of a much bigger plan and it had fuck-all to do with tackling hooliganism. Yet, I feel responsible, so again I apologise unreservedly.

Wait ... you didn't think I was apologising for any of my hooligan activities? We are evil ... we don't care.

The Football Disorder Act has such far-reaching powers it makes me fear for us all. Controversially, it gave the police powers to stop suspected soccer hooligans travelling abroad. *Suspected*! Have you ever been suspected of doing anything in your life that you know you didn't do? Of course you have; we've all said 'I never' or 'it wasn't me' and meant it. Well, this

Bill gives the State the right to stop you from travelling abroad on a suspicion. Officers are now able to stop anyone from leaving the country. That could be you. It definitely could be me. It's bad enough that they can prevent anyone from travelling anywhere (freedom of movement) to meet anyone (freedom of association) to chant whatever (freedom of expression) – but to give themselves the power to veto our right of innocence until proven guilty was nothing short of a criminal act by the State.

The Act gave police the power to arrest anyone they think may be travelling abroad to cause trouble at a match and take their passport off them. How open to abuse is that? Furthermore, how many people – both male and female – have a tattoo of their club or wear their football colours to the airport going on holiday, yet have never been involved in a single, solitary hooligan event in their lives? Is that you? Well, you are now a suspect. And suspects under this new Bill can then be taken to Court and banned from attending overseas matches for up to ten years. Ten years! Banned from travelling for ten years because of your tattoo and the new footie top you got for Christmas, because our State thinks and suspects that you might be guilty of a crime in the future. Stunning, truly fucking stunning – so endeth innocent until proven guilty. Worse, no crime has been committed. How do you plead innocent to a future crime?

'It wasn't me, guv ... fuck ... it didn't ... no ... I weren't there ... fuck ... shit ... I mean, I won't *be* there ... I'm not ever going there ... anyway, I wouldn't do that ... honest!' Tough. Guilty of a future, non-existent charge. The Thought Police said so and the Court ratified it. So the next time you are going on holiday during the season, cover your treasured club crest tattoo and keep the football shirts in the suitcase until you are pouring your sangria in the sun. Because it could be you.

A Lord Bassam felt it was right for police to have powers to stop people who are drunk or disorderly and check if they have a history of causing trouble at football matches. Well, no one is arguing with stopping people who are pissed, although running an on-the-spot history check suggested more technology, information storage and legislation would be in store. He said, 'It [the law] will give police additional powers to carry out their job. We think these powers are right and proportionate. Frankly, I think there is widespread public support for tough measures against those who want to destruct proper football fans.'

But the bill had fuck-all to do with tackling hooligans. Ministers even admitted that tattoos or what a fan was wearing could lead to their journey abroad being halted by the police. So they were admitting, too, that innocent people were going to be punished. That is why we stopped capital punishment. Innocent people swinging on the end of a rope. If innocent people are consistently found guilty then that's enough of that law. How many innocents will be convicted with this law? Yet the Government are happy with it. Why?

Hundreds and thousands of innocent people are going to fall victim to this law over the years. Guaranteed. So why are the legislators so happy with it? Because it is what they wanted. They like and need for us all to be afraid. It allows them to create more laws that ultimately will all have combined in totally eradicating all of our civil liberties and rights. We will live in fear, as is their wish. They continue to ply a police force already pissed on power with more muscle to control us. A police force whose previous record of wrongful convictions is hardly exemplary – Birmingham Six … Guildford Four. This at a time when we actually had rights, when we actually had a voice. I don't even want to imagine what the police force in a police State could do with impunity. Shoot innocent Brazilians half-a-dozen times from point-blank range maybe? Who knows.

Other laws have been passed to consolidate the State's position and further undermine ours. Our equivalent of the Patriot Act was passed in 2001. They rode the football hooligan vehicle a fair few clicks to eliminate plenty of our civil rights. They finished the job off with the Anti-Terrorist legislation. Somebody said, 'If you give up your civil rights for protection, you will end up with neither.' I may sound like some crazed conspiracy theorist – maybe I am. Oswald never pulled the trigger … 19 terrorists could not have pulled off 9/11 … there is no Easter Bunny and our Government is passing laws with the primary intention of eradicating all our civil rights. And for my part in the passing of the Football Disorder Act 2000, again, I apologise to the nation unreservedly.

So why – after establishing, allowing and encouraging our forefathers to let off steam from the 1880s all the way to 1968 – did they now decide to change our perspective on it? Why did they now want to outlaw this tradition for those who enjoyed and required it? Why ban hooligans now?

Is it because they want a placid, docile, thoughtless nation of zombies drip-fed on a diet of soaps, reality TV and football, which prevents us from asking questions of them and stops us fighting or even wanting to fight them? They want to take the sting from our tail, control our thoughts, actions, movements and lives. Combine what has been passed with what they still want to pass – i.e. legislation that allows the State to record, intercept and monitor all of our emails, text messages and mobile phone calls claiming it is for our homeland security. Do not believe it. And it's the same with ID cards. How would you and me having an ID card prevent one act of hooliganism or terrorism? It won't. Let us stand up to them as one. Ban hooligans? Fuck off. Let us become a nation of hooligans and fight back. Because if we don't start fighting back soon, a person in the not too distant future who wants to write some rabble-rousing, tub-thumping, get-the-peasants-revolting words like these, will not be allowed ... the Thought Police would have got to him already.

43

HUNGARY FOR A
EUROPEAN TEAR-UP

At last, 'We Are Evil' got to go on a European tour.
Manchester United had already qualified for the Champions
League, so after we played them in the 2004 FA Cup Final, we
had a pass into the UEFA Cup. We had been looking forward to
this since the semi-final victory, knowing when we had Man Utd
in the final that foreign soil was on. Dust off the passports.
Europe here we come!

This was going to be a test against an overseas team.
Hopefully, we would get Galatasaray or a big Italian club. The
day of the draw, Millwall fans were glued to Sky Sports or
listening to radios waiting to find out who we had. The news
came – Ferencvaros! Who the fuck are they? After a few phone
calls and a bit of Internet digging, we found out they were the
top club team in Hungarian football. Better than that, they also
had a hardcore hooligan firm with a long reputation.

In 1908, they intimidated Manchester United officials and
players so much during their month-long tour of Europe that
the club management said it would never return to Budapest
again. Sections of the crowd stoned the Manchester United team
and a near-riot broke out.

More recently, in July 2001, their firm had attacked Hadjuk Split fans in Budapest, stabbing one. A couple of years later, in May 2003, they failed to win their last game of the season, so failed to win the title. Their fans ran on the pitch and beat up their own coach, beat up some of their own players, then beat up some of the opposition players from Debrecen. And *we* are evil? We also learnt that they had given Newcastle fans a torrid time in 1996, attacking them all through the day in Budapest. It went from 'who the fuck are they?' to 'very promising' in no time at all.

We were due to play them at home for the first leg. That night, we were anticipating a good show. The invasion of a top European firm at The Den.

But fuck me, were we disappointed! They brought about 200 fans. That was it. Now I do not understand these European hooligans, or 'Ultras' as they call themselves. After all the trouble English fans have caused over the years, you would think that at least one would get their act together and come over here with a proper firm and have a go.

We played well, took the lead and led right up to the end. Unfortunately, they equalised in the last few minutes. The second leg was now set up nicely.

One of the chaps was knocking off a little bird in Thomas Cook. She had a right few tickets to book and sorted all our flights and hotels for Hungary. We were going all out on a five-day and four-night jaunt. It had taken over 100 years to qualify and it was likely to be the only time we ever would. The boat was getting well and truly pushed out. Fair play to the boys who follow their team throughout Europe every year, because our little trip cost us around £500, and another £400 on cocaine. I hadn't bought a pint yet and almost a grand had gone. Those who follow their teams in all the Champions League games must be doing £5,000–£10,000 a season. What a lovely problem to have. Oh, that would be money the vast majority of the firm would find for every game.

There were loads of eyes on us wanting to see us come unstuck. Other London firms and firms from all over the country, they all wanted to see us falling flat and take a hiding on foreign soil. Tuesday afternoon and we jetted off from Stansted, returning on the Saturday. Ten of us on our flight. Cab to the hotel, slung the bags in and right on the piss. Weather was lovely, a beautiful autumnal evening. We got slaughtered and, by the end of the night, I had done in half my charlie. The next day, another load of the boys arrived and we had taken over the third and fourth floors of the Domina Inn Hotel. More than 30 of us with another 30 downtown in the Ramada Budapest.

We were drinking down by the River Danube and there were a few isolated incidents with the locals. No big displays of hooliganism by any stretch. We are only hooligans when we see hooligans and are no trouble to people in regular situations. We had a big jolly-up and another all-day drinking session in a bar around the corner from the hotel. A couple of the boys ogled Juicy-Lucy the barmaid for the whole day. One or two of the locals took offence but every club that plays away is going to have a little fracas here and there. It was nothing really. We were all being ambassadors for the UK, and there were thousands of us there with virtually no trouble. Some estimates said 5,000 of us went, a lot without tickets, at a time when our average gates were 10,000. Put simply, every other person went to Hungary.

On the Thursday I rolled out of bed, and sort of missed breakfast. Two days on the piss meant a late rise on match day. Down to the Danube we headed. Everyone knew we were meeting down by the river, that was all pre-arranged. We got down there at about 3.00pm. Did not do too much eating. I don't actually remember going for one meal. We must have fucking ate, surely? Can't go four days without food ... surely? Went four days on cocaine; I know that. Took out my personal stash that lasted for about 24 hours. After that, one of the boys was coming round the hotel and dropping it off for us. In bulk. I suspect someone threw a couple of ounces up their arse and that is what we were snorting. Quality gear, even if it did have a funny smell to it. Thirty of us all tooting a couple of grams a day. Not worth buying three or four grams a day because cocaine is like fucking Pringles – once you start, you just can't stop. Whoever was selling it was a wise boy. So let me do a bit of maths here. Probably about 30 in our crew were on the charlie, with each one snorting two grams a day. One gram was 40 quid. (Obviously, we were buying our beer with the Hungarian florint but all coke was bought in sterling). Thirty men averaging two grams each at £80 a day ... £2,400!

Almost £2,500 a day, just from our crew alone. I thought he must run out of gear at some point, but did he fuck. Every time we belled him, within an hour he was there. I didn't know his face but, fair play to him, he kept us in charlie from the Wednesday evening right through until we went home. Not everyone was buying at the same time so he was running in and out of our hotel about four times every day, and probably four or five other bars and hotels every day, too. I do not know much he brought over but he never ran out of coke. We are talking thousands of Millwall boys tooting. The young kid was the front of it but some good brains were behind the whole operation. Somebody made a lot of money on cocaine off us over those few days.

So let me speculate again – 1,000 Millwall tooting for one day ... that's £80,000 *per day*! Somebody over a four-day period went back with a suitcase full of readies. It is the same at every home game, really. It helps. Hooligans like cocaine ... and Millwall hooligans love it.

By the day of the match, most of the firm had made it. A few of the boys were not allowed to fly due to the Old Bill checking everyone for warrants at the airports. Of the estimated 5,000 that were in Budapest, I heard a lot were without tickets. Of the firm? Well, we are possibly as many as 2,000-strong when everybody turns out. And everybody and their dog turned out. All the age range right from the young ones to 60-plus. Not hooligans on the first two nights, just tourists en masse enjoying a good few drinks on a couple of beautiful evenings in Hungary.

It was now the day of the match and trouble was expected. There was a different feeling in the air that day as we set ourselves up in a few bars near the River Danube. There was a little scuffle between a group of young Millwall from different areas – Peckham and Bermondsey. Nothing major, just a little difference of opinion; other than that, it had been completely trouble free. Late afternoon, we saw a mob of about 30 Ultras at the end of the road. They came running down the road at us. It was match day and the Ultras had landed. This was what we had come for. Running down the road at us ... Millwall. Noise? Oh yes. It sounded to me like some bizarre Hungarian war chant. Weapons? Oh yes.

They had baseball bats and sticks. And bottle? Oh no. We charged them and they turned and ran. That was our introduction to the Ultras on their own turf. Imagine if the boot had been on the other foot. Millwall charging and then turning and running. No. I can't imagine that either.

The rest of the afternoon was followed by spotters coming down and looking but there were no more attacks. All hoodies and jeans they had been, although, in all honesty, I am not sure exactly what they were wearing because they didn't get close enough. We carried on drinking in the bars and, by now, there were thousands of us milling around.

The evening came and it was time to head to the ground, we made our way from the riverside bars up to the Underground station. There were about 500 of us looking for a ruck. There was no Old Bill to be seen anywhere as we crossed Vorosmarty Square, a big, central square that had four roads leading off it, one from each corner. As we reached the top left-hand corner, the Ultras came running up one of the side roads. They obviously had a plan to trap us in the square. Without hesitation, we ran towards them. They all had scarves wrapped around their faces and were carrying all sorts of weapons – lumps of wood, chains and iron bars. One of them at the front was swinging a big lump of wood about. One of our boys punched him and knocked him to the floor; he picked up his weapon and started hitting him with it. He took some punishment with his own weapon that boy, getting smacked in the face and the head a right few times. This caused panic in their ranks and they began running off in all directions. We began to pick them off. I picked a few off. One was sprinting past; I threw a right hook. He stumbled. I kicked his ankles to trip him up, then kicked fuck out of him on the floor. Two others joined in and they kicked fuck out of him, too. He took some heavy boots to the face and head. Claret was running all down his face and he was curled into a little ball. He'd had enough.

We are not fighting to the death here. You just know when someone has had enough. It may be one kick. Often one punch is the final punch if you catch them right. Ex-boxers know. That boy had had enough. I moved on, looking for more action. They had all scattered. A group of what looked like bouncers came running into the square, all Grant Mitchell clones with shaved heads and bomber jackets. The hoodies had already run back down the road they had come from. Everyone's attention turned to the meatheads. As we got near them, they managed to position themselves in front of a temporary bar in the square.

This was the second wave of Ultras. There had been no indication this was going to happen. I was supercharged now, but could not get near them as already about 30 of our firm surrounded about 20 of these bouncers. They come under a barrage of chairs and tables before the fists and feet started flying. We had them totally trapped and they took a severe beating. Most of them were on the floor taking a right kicking to their heads, bodies and into their bollocks. The Reeboks were raining in as a few of them managed to run away. Their tactic of backs to the bar had backfired on them big time. A few were cut off before they could join their meathead mates. Lucky them.

Then the first sighting of the Old Bill. Four cars pulled into the pedestrianised square and saved the meatheads from any more punishment. Four cars with four in each, 16 Old Bill. All the police carry guns over there. Time to move on.

We continued to the Underground, really pumped up now. Three days of drinking with no proper food, three days of charlie with no proper food, three separate little incidents where I had been throwing punches and kicking fuck out of a few of these Ultras. Oh yes! We were pumped up all right on that walk to the Underground.

As we headed up the road from the square to Vorosmarty Metro station, virtually every shop window was put through. Big department stores with big shop fronts, maybe 30 shops. It was between 6.00-7.00pm so all the shops were closed, luckily for them. We are evil, we are evil. Everything in our way was getting smashed up now. After all the shop windows were put through, café chairs and tables were smashed. Alarms were going off everywhere.

We finally reached the Underground and boarded the train thinking that we'd had our fun for the day. Little did we know there was a surprise waiting for us. As we headed for the stadium, the train journey was a normal one. People laughing, cracking jokes and replaying tales of what had happened in the square. There were four stops before we reached the stadium. As the train pulled into the first station, the doors stayed shut.

No one sensed anything. No one guessed what was about to happen. We were all on that one train in about four or five coaches, all packed in tight. The platform of Ferenciek tere was empty. Eerily empty. Something definitely was not right. Then from nowhere, a mob of them come running on to the platform armed with baseball bats. One at the front was carrying a machete. They tried to smash the train windows and doors through. It was mental inside the train with everyone trying to get out. We managed to pull the doors open and piled off. They did not know Millwall.

The machete boy and his intimidatory tactics did not work. The machete boy didn't injure one of us. It happened so quick. No fear! No food! Lots of coke! Lots of alcohol! Lots of adrenalin! That boy's machete got us even more hyped. There were about 20 of them that I could see. Don't know how many more at each carriage. They backed off straight away and, once we got the doors open, we attacked. They didn't know what had hit them and clearly expected us to stay cowering inside the train. The ones at the front got steam-rollered and knocked down. The rest turned and ran straight back up the escalators. They had just come down to attack us; now they were fighting each other to get up the stairs.

Some of our lads had reached them on the escalators and

were throwing them down the stairs. We were down the bottom bashing fuck out of them as they landed at our feet. They were getting kicked, stamped and punched on the floor. As one landed, one of our firm picked him up by the collar and pinned him to the wall. I must have punched him ten times. He was in a bit of a state. He was not knocked out but he did some groaning. Each time I hit him, what was I thinking? 'Fuck! I don't want to miss! Not with that wall behind.' What a noise that thud of knuckle on cheek makes. He turned his head and the rest caught him on the side of the face. One eye over your shoulder at all times. The boy holding him hit six or seven times. That boy took some punishment. I have wondered if that was his last ever day as a Hungarian football hooligan. That is enough to put you off. I have never taken punishment like that. Plenty of times I have been tagged and taken punches but never punishment like that. Not sure if I would have been out for the next battle if I had taken that beating. At least you must start having thoughts like, 'It didn't say this on the tin ... it definitely didn't say this on the tin. Why the fuck did I get involved in this in the first place?'

Having said that, I do not know of one Millwall fan that stopped his association with the firm after taking a beating. Not one. Know plenty that have taken a severe beating but not one that ever packed in. Not one. They would all come back for the next round. Maybe some of the young ones do not come back; sure, lots have tried it and it just was not for them.

There was a big column in the middle of the platform. One Ferencvaros Ultra was stood at the side of the column. He was squaring up with one of our boys. They were both hesitating. I didn't ... I punched him on the side of the head with a right. He stumbled over and was about to hit the floor. Our boy jumped straight on him and pummelled him. His head was bouncing on the floor. I ran round the column. They had gone. Ultras? Ultra quick at running, I will give them that.

We left the platform littered with bodies and re-boarded the train. It must have lasted three to four minutes. They had been heavily tooled up with baseball bats, the machete boy and lumps of wood – big, fuck-off lumps of four-by-two. It could have been more of a fight but once the ones at the front were dropped, the other 30 were obviously disheartened by the loss of their leaders and ran. Millwall have no leaders. We are never gonna have that feeling of 'Oh no, our leader is down … what do we do now?' Probably a big factor in why we have been the top firm for so long.

As we reached the next station at Nepliget, again we had a reception. We were wiser. Waiting for them waiting for us! It was a carbon copy of the last time. We pulled the doors open and jumped off, again they were tooled up but they did not put up much of a fight. Once the ones at the front got dropped, the ones at the back ran. We got back on the train knowing we had a couple more stops before the stadium.

The train pulled in to the next one. We were ready for another greeting but this time all was quiet. Same at the next and then it was the stadium stop. We made our way out of the station and were met by riot police. They had one of the exits blocked, forcing us all out of the other one. As we turned the corner, we spotted some Ultras in a bar to our right, so we headed to the door to get into the bar. I was trying to get in the pub. One of us kicked the door. Locked. I was ready to go through that door, this was the frontline. I was charged … supercharged. A fight in the square … a fight at the train station … a fight at the next train station. Now I am ready to pile into their main pub. This was a whole new fucking scenario now.

I am ready … I am Millwall … We are evil.

Then – gas. The Hungarian police have adopted their own tactics to stop us. Gas us. CS gas. That first breath ... your throat is on fire ... your lungs ... it is like pepper ... but times it by a fucking gazillion ... your eyes go, then your nose, anything and everything wet is in pain. It is a burning sensation and you cannot breathe. There were ten of us around the door trying to get in. I was frontline and got gassed in the face. Everybody following through that walkway was affected – this shit sticks in the air. We are evil but that CS gas is pure evil. Hundreds of us were coughing and spluttering. For a good few minutes, even from ten yards away, the big fire extinguisher CS canisters are naughty. Very naughty. One squirt did the damage. Took ten of us out for ten minutes. I knew when I saw that canister what was in store. Once I had been fucking about with one of them when just a kid in the back garden. Oh, I knew what was in store.

We ran out of the exit into the fresh air. Once the eyes cleared we were still reeling from the gas, spitting, coughing and spluttering. One kid was vomiting but it did not set anybody else off, no gag reflex with anybody. To our right was another group of Ultras jumping up and down and waving us forward. From the side, one of our lads ran into them and, with a peach of a punch, sent one crashing to the floor. We ran towards them but the riot police prevented us from getting close. My eyes were still streaming but I was ready to go again. We were hemmed, penned and herded towards the ground but we made a run at them; again, to our disappointment, they turned tail and ran. The police finally got us into the ground.

The match itself went to Ferencvaros. We put up a good fight on the field, too, but lost 4–2 on aggregate. It was a decent game with a cracking atmosphere. We were in it at the start but only for a while. Paul Ifill missed a good chance early on and 'Wall were containing Ferencvaros well, and offering attacking options. But the momentum swung decisively in favour of the Hungarians with a header from a cross from the right flank. They actually scored then three times in fifteen minutes to take control of the tie. Game over. Wise pulled one back on the stroke of half time after a Dave Livermore (Bermondsey's Zidane) fluffed shot fell to him. Half time. 4–2 on aggregate.

We did put up a battling second-half performance but we were unable to score. Harris hit the side-netting from a corner. We also hit the woodwork twice. If we could have scored one in the second half, it would have been squeaky bum time for them with the away goals rule but it just was not to be. At least we were in it and they gave us plenty to sing and shout about.

During the match, we heard that three Millwall fans had been stabbed; none of our mob but some scarfers in separate incidents. You seem to hear this a lot with foreign hooligans. Always gunning for the supporters wearing colours and stabbing them. Anyone in Britain wearing team colours is off limits. We are only hooligans with other hooligans.

After the game, the police escorted us out, straight back on the Tube and back to the River Danube we were sent. Felt a bit for one bar owner. We'd had a good piss-up in his bar the day before, about 20 of us had had a right few pints, not as hooligans. Unfortunately, his bar got in the way of trouble.

There was no more trouble that night, though. We got back to our hotel and heard the Ultras would be looking for revenge. They never showed! Back at the hotel that night, it was more drinking and more tooting. Most stayed on the Thursday night and ten of us stayed on the Friday night. More drinking ... more tooting ... ambassadors again. No trouble.

Oh, to have qualified for Europe every season. Oh, to have got through against Ferencvaros. We would have entered the group stages of the UEFA Cup. Two games at home and two away. Feyenoord of Rotterdam ... Schalke 04 of Gelsenkirchen ... Basel of Switzerland ... and Hearts of Edinburgh. You were all lucky firms in lucky cities.

44

THE FIGURES DON'T LIE ... DO THEY?

Police reckon they are battling a new breed of football hooligan now because a report revealed a rise in the number of arrests at football games. Of course it did – because they expanded massively the definition of hooliganism, ensuring more football-related arrests. In the Eighties, the Tories would manipulate unemployment figures to make things look better than they were. 16- to 18-year-olds weren't included. Excellent. Half a million less unemployed with the stroke of a mighty pen. People with green eyes – don't count them, either. Super. Down to 3.2 million on the dole. Police are now doing the opposite to make football hooliganism look a lot worse than it actually is.

A National Criminal Intelligence Service (NCIS) report showed 3,391 people were arrested for football-related offences in 2001 – up 8.1 per cent on the previous year. Yet examine the figures and it's clear that only 137 were for assault and 165 for affray. Nearly 2,300 were for being pissed and gobby. That is not football hooliganism, that is being pissed and gobby. We all see it every night out we go on. It's got fuck-all to do with football hooliganism.

Around one million people go to watch football every week,

for 40 weeks of the year. That's around 40 million a year. And a couple of hundred were arrested. 'The English disease', they say. Hardly a fucking epidemic, is it? They know what they're doing with these figures, so the question is: Why do they want to make it look ten times worse than it is? Ten times! And that is giving them the huge benefit of the doubt that the 165 for affray and the 137 for assault were all found guilty. The report found 'there has been a shift in the focus of the violence, with the vast majority of incidents occurring away from the matches themselves'. I would love to interview them on this topic.

'Present is a known football hooligan and PC241 and Detective No Truth. It is 6.00pm. These incidents away from the matches, they're still near the ground, though, right?'

'Define near.'

'Within a mile or two.'

'We-ell … not really.'

'Just after the game, though, right?'

'Define just.'

'Within an hour or two.'

'We-ell … not really.'

'So in a different town and a couple of days later?'

'No comment.'

The report went on: 'Hooligans are becoming more organised, using mobile phones and the Internet to communicate with each other.' The whole fucking world is actually. But we like to talk and email, too, you know. We do not spend all day punching others. Got to have a little chat to break up the monotony of punching and kicking.

NCIS admitted, 'Violence inside all-seater stadiums is virtually non-existent.' So why do they want to paint a picture of every town and city dripping in the blood and guts of thousands of innocent bystanders on a match day. Why? Is it because it is a top earner for them that has increased massively as billions have been ploughed into the game?

Brian Drew, head of specialist operations at NCIS, said, 'There is a nasty, ugly and anti-social element in society that clings parasitically to football and just won't give up.' Brian has just perfectly described the Old Bill there ... or was it just me?

'What became the English disease is no longer characterised by the mass terrace affrays and running street battles that we saw in the 1970s and 1980s but, like other infections, new strains of football hooliganism are developing that are clever, resilient and increasingly resistant.' New strains ... developing ... resilient ... what the ... ? Am I a hooligan, a whooping cough or fucking bird 'flu? But seeing as we are no longer viewed as just brainless, meathead thugs, I set aside my confusion and questions to prove indeed that I was clever, resilient and increasingly resistant by finishing Mr Drew's report. It confirmed that the Football Disorder Act was helping to tackle the problem. So everyone can sleep safely in the knowledge that a White Paper wiped out hooliganism, right? Because 'more than 518 people were banned from visiting football matches at home and abroad under the legislation in the first year alone'.

Not enough for Mr Drew, because he 'would like to see police and magistrates make more rigorous use of their powers'. You don't think they already make enough frighteningly overwhelming, we-can-do-what-the-fuck-we-please-how-and-when-we-choose, rigorous use of their powers? We live in a police State. What more do you want?

'The major area of concern is the ability to travel to other towns and cities with the prime intention of committing crime, whether that be violence, disorderly behaviour or, as we now know, drug dealing.' Drug dealing! What the fuck has that got to do with football hooliganism? You may as well lump terrorists in with handbag snatchers. Enough of this shit. What are you really trying to tell us and what do you really want?

'[The Act] confers a discretionary power on the Court to impose additional requirements when imposing a banning order.' You mean you have given the State the authority to do whatever it wants to anyone in a Court of law. Well, all our civil rights and liberties are already up in smoke so come on, Mr Drew, what are you really after for the State that the State has not already taken from us?

'With the spread of pay-per-view TV, and TV dictating when certain matches are played, such as with an evening kick-off when people have been drinking all day, there is a lot of money in football which police forces would benefit from accessing.' Sure they would, yes. So let me see if I have got this right – you want Millwall to give you my entrance fee to the match so you can put more police on duty to increase your chances of coshing me over the head? Seems fair. Shall I send my season ticket cheque direct to the Metropolitan Police then just pop round every Saturday for a quick coshing, Mr Drew? Would that be the best way for you?

So that is what it is all about – money. Money, money, money. I knew it; I fucking knew it. Paint the blackest and bleakest of pictures first, terrify everyone into thinking it is Armageddon every Saturday, then wring every penny out of the clubs that you can. Billions in football today, right? The State wants its share of the pie! After all, if you want a Police State, someone has got to pay. You can't tax a football fan for going to the match directly but another surreptitious, indirect tax, no problem. In fact, fucking ingenious. Hope whoever thought of that got a promotion. Guess the profit is all commission-based only. So if ten Old Bill are needed for three hours, you clear £10 per hour per man off each club. But if you tell the clubs they are going to need, ooh, let's say 1,200 Old Bill on duty, plus 100 horses, 50 dogs (top commission on them) 50 vans, 30 bikes and a chopper for 10 hours or the game can't be played for safety reasons, then that club has to fork out a fortune to 'pay you off' or they will lose a whole lot more. Brilliant. You have got the clubs bent over a barrel with their trolleys around their ankles, haven't you? No wonder Dave Whelan at Wigan almost took you to Court.

And who pays in the end anyway? Us, the fans. The ones that keep the turnstiles clicking. I paid for the fucking new cosh that twatted me over the back of the head, which was in the hands of some Old Bill whose wages I already pay towards. What a mug. It is not only the clubs you have got bent over a barrel, is it? Fucking knew I should have started that barrel business in Bermondsey. Bastards!

45

SO I SUPPOSE A RUCK'S OUT OF THE QUESTION, THEN?

It had been a long time since we had played Leeds United. Not one of our big rivals by any stretch. They had their Service Crew back in the Eighties but a big police operation took them out of commission, really. They'd had that trouble in Galatasaray in Europe and they still had their hooligan element; from our perspective, we were expecting a big reception and hoping for opportunities to break the police cordon.

Sure, we sold our ticket allocation for the match in October 2007, and probably about 3,000 of us went up. Nothing pre-arranged; nothing has to be. Everyone just knows that everyone is going. The station was packed with the usual faces. A good drink at London Bridge to begin with and, of course, the usual smuggling the drinks on. Dry trains? Not so dry, really. The old days had gone where you could buy a few cans on the train. For years, cans of beer littered the tables; now on dry trains it is big lemonade and Coca-Cola bottles that are scattered everywhere. A couple of hours getting up there had us vodka-fuelled at Leeds Central.

A sea of Old Bill as we are getting off the train. A sea of them – horses, dogs, riot police, vans – all the usual. They held us outside the station. It filters through that they have a load of buses to shunt us to Elland Road. Happy days. Normally, we would just be frog-marched from a station to a ground. Very kind of Yorkshire Police. And how do we repay the kindness of the local constabulary? On arriving at Elland Road, we smashed the windows and kicked open the doors of the double-decker buses, attempting to incite the home supporters.

The first few windows on our bus got kicked through because the Old Bill were not letting us off. They were getting twitchy ... very twitchy. Leeds fans were trying to get at us and we were trying to get off the bus. Wicked combination. The Old Bill had their hands full all right. This must have gone on for a couple of minutes.

Once the windows on the bus were going through, the Old Bill were getting even more edgy. So they cleared a big path by pushing all the Leeds fans to one side, locked a load of them in their own club shop, and off the bus we got. Hundreds and hundreds of Old Bill. No one was breaking any cordons. A few little skirmishes with them as a few of our boys were trying to get out. But again, no one was breaking the police cordon. No missiles, no skirmishes with Leeds. They just piled us into the ground and it was virtually kick-off time.

During the game, across the other side from me, a few of our boys got through the stewards and the police. A handful piled into the Leeds fans, who all backed off. It looked like a few punches were thrown by our boys but the Leeds fans didn't want to know, so Millwall clambered back into our section, although it looked like one or two of them got nicked. Big atmosphere, though, and it looked like a full house. We were loud and certainly played our part in creating the hostile and intimidating atmosphere that carried on for the full game. More than our players did in creating a contest in the match itself.

Full-time whistle went – 4–2. Four down after an hour, a bad day at the office.

Held in the ground – as usual. Probably about 20–30 minutes just chatting among ourselves. The thousands of Leeds fans had virtually disappeared by the time they let us out. A handful of tough guys had stuck around to give us the usual hand gestures. Nothing more than that. We were all piling out of the stadium. Again, hundreds and hundreds of Old Bill – riot police, vans, dogs. But no coaches for us. We were virtually last out. Maybe a few at the front had been ferried away on buses. I don't know. All the buses were demolished and undrivable when I looked back at them before entering the ground.

We were marched a long old trot back to the station. Seemed like for ever. We had been out early that day and stood up throughout the game. Throw in a good drink before with a few lines of Charlie, then you stop drinking and sober up. Throw in a good whacking on the pitch and a walk around the corner would have seemed like a half-marathon. This walk back to Leeds station seemed to take an age, but I bet no one was thinking, 'Wish we never smashed them buses up now.' They were just a bonus lifting us into the ground in the first place.

Going back to the station was the usual frog-march and the Old Bill had dispersed all of the Leeds fans. It had been a massive police operation on that day and Leeds got nowhere near us. Not too many wise people want to get nicked in any situation and the first ones trying to break through a police cordon are often nicked. It may be difficult to imagine 3,000 being hemmed in or 30,000 Leeds being blocked out but riot police, thousands of them, mounted police, specially trained forces, helicopters with cameras and spotlights, spotters with cameras filming before, during and after, CCTV in and around the ground ... believe me, they can hold two sets of fans apart.

And what a massive expense, all for a couple of hours of football. All to keep two sets of fans apart. Half the time, the Old Bill create more trouble than they prevent. I have seen the Internet footage of the Leeds fans rioting into the night. Did the police create more trouble than they would have prevented? Well, on a night like that – it sure looks like it to me. If they hadn't been there, we would have met the Leeds fans and given them a good kicking. They would have turned tail and that would have been that. See you next season and all over in a couple of minutes. They rioted against the police for hours and caused untold damage and injuries. Will Old Bill never learn?

We got back from Leeds station after not one of our better days out. All piled off the train at King's Cross and headed for a boozer. Only one thing to do after a day like that – get pissed again. In The Gregorian Arms, we drowned our sorrows and drank the night away.

It had already fully dawned on me that this was football today. Massive police operations with not much chance of a good drink and a tear-up. Just herded in and herded out and filmed all day on camera. If I had wanted that I would have gone into acting. The good old days increasingly appeared to be gone for ever. Millwall and away days were not the fun they used to be. Every big game is 'potentially explosive' to the Old Bill. Even the small ones are deemed that way, too. I can't believe any other teams are treated like us. We know the term 'bubble-wrapped' and, for sure, in some of the Premiership games the away fans are bubble-wrapped. But us at Millwall? We are tied up, gagged, bound, bubble-wrapped, stuck inside a box, inside a safe, re-wrapped ... with a little fucking bow stuck on top. Going away with Millwall was now a military operation for the police and it meant getting to and from the ground with no ability to move or even go for a pint. Rioting with the police is not what it's about for me – a good game of football with a good piss-up and a good ruck. On this day, all three were sadly missing.

We met Leeds again in a 2009 play-off semi-final. A second-leg ticket at Elland Road was only available to season ticket holders. We had to buy a voucher from Millwall, then on the day of the match we had to get to Woolley Edge service station to pick up our ticket from the police while we were being filmed. There was no trouble.

46

BLACK, WHITE
AND BLUE

When the Met launch an undercover operation the first location they come up with is The Den. This time was no different as they targeted football hooligans who use racist chants and abuse black players. They would have got much better results going to Chelsea, who have been strongly linked with Combat 18, a right-wing, racist group. One geezer actually joined their firm from Cardiff because of C18. Racism has never been a big issue at Millwall but the Met headed over to us anyway, unsurprisingly. They would certainly have got better results with an undercover operation at their own HQ, given the institutional racism in the Metropolitan Police.

They carried out the first two operations, in which dozens of officers were used to secretly record and photograph offensive chanting, in late 1998. They could have picked any club and got the same results. These things are all done for a reason, of course, but – no offence intended to any black person – but this was not done to protect you. The initiative came about because the Home Office was set to announce proposals for stiffer penalties against hooligans at football matches. It just needed a new report to justify them. A stricter vetting programme to try to control the type of people following the England team abroad was then subsequently unveiled by the Football Association. Sir Paul Condon, Metropolitan Police Commissioner at the time, apparently showed films of the two undercover operations, both obviously involving followers of Millwall. When you need maximum exposure for some new civil-liberty-busting imminent legislation, then use the biggest bad boy in town. An old, transparent tactic.

In one, five men aged 19–42 were recorded and filmed making monkey noises and chanting racist obscenities by undercover police officers. Condon admits the investigation, known as Operation Den, was intended to make people afraid that 'the police could be recording them at any match'. He described their behaviour as 'despicable and offensive'. Under the Home Office clampdown, measures included making the chanting of racist abuse by an individual fan a criminal offence. Fair enough. Not too many enlightened people at the start of the new millennium would oppose the eradication of racism, in all walks of life, not just football.

Yet what they tagged on the end of it can only lead anyone to believe that targeting racists and protecting the black community was the last thing on their mind. To begin with, a racist and a hooligan are two entirely separate beings. For hooligan read 'delinquent', 'hoodlum', 'lout', 'ruffian', 'tearaway', 'thug', 'tough', 'troublemaker', 'vandal' and 'yob'. For racist, read 'biased, 'bigoted', 'chauvinistic', 'discriminatory', 'intolerant', 'prejudiced' and 'xenophobic'. Even using the *Oxford Popular Thesaurus*, there is not one word that crosses over or links a racist with a hooligan. The reason is simple: they are totally different. The vast majority of hooligans would be offended at being called a racist, myself included. I would hazard a guess that not too many KKK members ever went to a football game for a good old punch-up and a piss-up. Too busy cutting holes out of their stupid fucking pointy hats. For sure, some people are both; without doubt, there are racist hooligans but, without doubt, they are in the minority. Yet the hood-winkers at the Home Office lump it all together to achieve their main objectives.

The Home Office had a hidden agenda and used Commissioner Condon as their vehicle. He used football – and, in particular, Millwall – as his vehicle. He launched Operation Den, ostensibly to ban racism at football. Records were taken and five people were arrested – a landslide victory. And so the propaganda machine was let loose – the press were called in to inform the public dutifully and obligingly about the 'outrage' at Millwall. The public accepted it all unquestioningly, as we invariably do. The legislation was passed. The vehicles had all been ridden smoothly on their way to a final destination.

So under the guise of tackling racism, a noble cause, of course, legislation was soon introduced that contained new laws which would bring in more revenue through higher fines and exclusion orders – designed to prevent people from travelling abroad because they do not like your tattoo or bald head or football shirt or designer jumper or your face; in effect, they now had the ability to ban anyone from going to any game and gained more control over the sales of tickets for matches overseas. Bang went freedom of speech, freedom of movement, freedom of association and innocent until proven guilty. Never mind hooliganism; civil liberties would soon be a thing of the past.

The Government's Working Group on Football-Related Disorder wanted 'greater effort by clubs, their stewards and police to tackle racist chanting and remarks'. Again, just completely pass the buck – why not? They also wanted to see 'initiatives to recognise and develop the value of grassroots football as a method of promoting social inclusion'. Sounds great, that, but what you are really saying, though, is just get kids playing football so they don't feel left out. Kids have been doing that up and down the country on their own since Dick docked. Good effort, though, and you have to publish something after all those hours sat around talking shite.

There have been a number of high-profile campaigns to drive out racism from football, by the clubs, Government, police and the PFA. The Professional Footballers' Association and the Commission for Racial Equality founded the 'Kick It Out' campaign. It gives children the opportunity to see footballers talking personally about the effect of racism on their lives. Great idea – it can help break the cycle of racism being taught or passed on through every generation. I am all for it.

Other clubs came up with their own ideas to combat the problem. Derby County teamed up with the police in a scheme called Rams Against Football Troublemakers. Sheffield Wednesday and police regularly exchange information about known hooligans to ensure that anyone banned from the ground for causing trouble is kept away from games. Not sure how or if it works, but I would assume that the threat of it could keep some away. They want everyone to feel like they are being watched all the time.

They also have a scheme under which suspected hooligans can be banned before they are proven guilty. Let me repeat: under the initiative, the club can ban fans before the Courts convict them! That could be any Wednesday fan who is casually strolling around on a nice, sunny day with a tin in her hand a mile from the ground. Bang ... you're nicked. Tagged, bagged and banned before your beer is warm, by the club you have supported all your life, pressured by a Government who is telling us that the loss of our fundamental right to innocent until proven guilty is for our benefit – to eradicate the hooligan problem. It is just the contempt they have for us. It is natural. We all know that. I don't even take it personally anymore.

Some lies are despicable and intended to frighten us and to take us to war – Saddam has WMDs; terrorists are in your street and flying overhead right now. Some are funny – in the run-up to Euro 2000, the Home Office said that domestic hooliganism was over. Oh, right. Then what the fuck are a couple of thousand riot cops lurking with intent outside my living room window for every other Saturday? As he himself said, the bigger the lie, the more people believe it. And this – give up your right to innocence so that we may protect you even better – is as big a lie as you will ever hear.

Forgetting I am a hooligan anyway, surely everyone has got to be concerned by the fact that you now only have to be 'suspected'. Glad I'm not a Wednesday fan. The club and South Yorkshire Police claimed this strategy was to tackle violence, racism and anti-social behaviour both inside and outside the ground. Of course, the Old Bill are behind it, they have a vested interest.

Apparently, the Wednesday Against Soccer Hooligans scheme (WASH) 'has helped make improvements to safety inside the ground and other measures are planned'. Lord knows what else they introduced or what other measures they have planned. Tag everyone? Chip in their forearm to track them? Camera in their living room to record them? And they are just putting the finishing touches to a machine that reads minds.

Fucking hell. Scary shit. They only want to watch a game of football. No wonder Wednesday's gate receipts have fallen through the floor.

47

SINKING FEELING AFTER 'DAMAGING' HULL

We jumped an early train from King's Cross. It was a long old journey but, because we were unusually early, we could have a few beers on the train. It was about 6.00–7.00 on a cold January morning in 2009, and they were the only tickets we could get. It got to opening time and more than 30 of us found a pub in the centre of Hull not far from the station. Stayed drinking for hours in just a normal, regular Hull pub with a couple of nice barmaids. A few Hull fans came in wearing shirts. No animosity given by us. Scarfers are out of bounds for us. Must have spent about four hours in that bar having a good laugh with no trouble at all. Thirty-odd Millwall all spending big money. They probably took a grand off us in those few hours.

We finally made our way out and the police were milling around everywhere. The early-early train meant we avoided the usual shite but, once out of the pub, the police were waiting for us, although not a heavy escort. There were only a few of us and we went straight into the ground. A few coachloads of private buses were already in and the bulk of the fans were on later trains. We heard that a load of Millwall had rampaged and steamed through a shopping centre. Obviously, a bit of a shock for the afternoon shoppers but, from what I heard, nothing too major. Heard, too, that a few had steamed into some Hull outside a pub. Again, nothing major.

All the Millwall fans were in by kick-off. Just before the match started, all the netting that they put up to separate the fans was trampled over. Then a few went over to Hull. I think one punch was thrown – don't think it connected. The match started with coins and lighters going back and forth. A few 'Wall must have run out of money and clippers because a few seats then went flying over to the Hull side. Not sure if they smashed up seats, too, but a few definitely came back at us. We were constantly goading each other back and forth but still nothing major – just the usual. A hostile atmosphere with a bit of shit flying to and fro. And that was it. Game finished with a 2–0 defeat for us. Nothing happened.

We were all heading home thinking, 'Bollocks, out the Cup and all round a quite uneventful away day.' It had been a long old day but I managed to force myself for a couple of pints down The Quays – The Warrior as was, The Tavern now. Got home totally done in. Woke up Sunday, had a full English and a stroll down the shops for the papers. Fucking hell! Was that the same boring day out we'd been on the day before?

Hull City chairman Paul Duffen demanded that Millwall provide full compensation for the damage caused. A statement that appeared on the Hull website condemned the actions of us away fans. It read: 'It is already clear that a significant contingent of the travelling Millwall supporters arrived at the match with a single intention of causing maximum disruption.'

The pick of the press reports included: 'There were violent scenes during the Hull v Millwall game at Hull's KC Stadium

...'; 'Large numbers of rival fans ripped up seats during the match, which they used as missiles during Hull's 2–0 win ...'; and 'Photographs of 32 suspected hooligans were published shortly after the trouble and the images appeared on the Most Wanted section of the Crimestoppers website. Members of the public are urged to view the pictures and help police identify those involved.'

Crimestoppers said it was the first time photographs of suspected football hooligans had been published on the website. Dave Cording, the organisation's Director of Operations, said, 'We are urging the public to help the police by identifying these individuals who were involved in disrupting this football match. Unfortunately, there still exists an unpleasant minority of fans whose intention it is to cause criminal damage and incite violence.'

Honestly, what a boring, quiet day out it had been. I mean, really. A few Millwall boys giving it the old Johnny Depp in *Pirates of the Caribbean* by making cut-throat gestures, a couple more using the seats as boomerangs and a few piss-holes being smashed is hardly the stuff of Luton '85. Of course, the press embellishment that has followed Millwall persists today, just like it always has. Perhaps, God forbid, it really isn't as bad as so many articles want to make out.

'IT WAS A LOVELY PEACEFUL GAME THAT FINISHED 2–2 AND EVERYONE WENT HOME HAPPY WITH FOOTBALL AS THE WINNER' wouldn't sell as many copies of the *News on Sunday* as 'MILLWALL MORONS DO IT AGAIN!' Just a guess. But drop the dead donkey because somebody was caught smoking in the toilets at The New Den today!

And that is how many Millwall fans feel, rightly or wrongly. That is how we feel. It was all a pile of bullshit and completely blown out of proportion. But I guess it's only what we have come to expect.

48

HOOLIE HEAVEN

Consider everything the authorities have done attempting to stop the problem of hooliganism – yet nothing seems to work. If two firms really want to have a go at each other, then there is not much else all the relevant parties can introduce that they haven't already. And still the problem persists. Football hooligans in the main don't hate each other. OK – we hate West Ham; and there's no love lost between Tottenham v Arsenal, Celtic v Rangers, City v United, Liverpool v United ... OK, pretty much everyone v United. Yes. They and others all hate each other. But the rest, the others, you just want to fight with them because they are fellow hooligans. No more than that.

When a team is free of a hooligan element then there will be no trouble that day. Obviously, West Ham and us go back to the very beginnings of league football. It is a deep-rooted, deep-seated, generational, virtually genetic condition. Everyone else, we just want to fight them because they want to fight us. If they have no one to fight us, or if they never wanted to fight us, there would be no fights. Obviously that works both ways. We want to fight them and they want to fight us. We all love a good punch-up. And that is football hooliganism.

The definition of hooliganism has changed, remember. Nowadays, gesticulating and holding a tin an hour before the game a mile away from the ground and you are a hooligan. So from someone that has been on the inside of this for many a long year, how about listening to my – somewhat radical – suggestion to combat the problem of hooliganism?

Legalise it.

That's right. Legalise football hooliganism. Fucking simple, eh? Legalise it. And that way it is not a problem.

Here is the effect. All the clubs would save a fortune as policing costs would fall through the floor. With the money we promise to save them, they promise to build in each community a Hoolidron or a Hoolidrome, a sort of cauldron for us hooligans if you will. Fuck, we would even chip in for it and pay our subs – £1 per week, per hoolie.

On match day, however many the away firm bring is the size of the battle. No. Hang on, it's all organised before. The National Committee of Hooligans is established to run the Hooli-Leagues (Divisions 1–4). They also formalise the rules, e.g. a 20-minute, total free-for-all. Sides limited to 200 per team. No half-times. No weaponry of any type allowed. One side only becomes the winners when the opposition firm have all left the field of play. If after 20 minutes there appears to be a stalemate, then each side will nominate five from their firm to fight in the five-minute extra-time period. Each firm that wins gets three points. Bonus point for every knock-out. Bonus points for speed of victory. One point for every minute within the twenty that victory is secured by. There could be some preliminary rounds. The so-called top boys from each firm would meet. Don't know what we would do – pick any ten from a big, big number. It would not matter to us. Three points to the winner.

The toe-to-toe round (ten names go in a hat and one is picked).

The ten v ten round (twenty names go in a hat and ten are picked).

The ton v ton round (where a ton of man fights a ton of man from their firm. Numbers don't matter in this round, you've just got to weigh in at a ton. Each winner from each contest gets three points).

Points deducted if everyone is dressed identically. Bonus points if the away firm is bigger than the home firm for league games.

And the final round – the free-for-all. Two hundred v two hundred – all pile into a specially built ring, and anyone who has had enough has to make it to the sin-bin and, once there, he can't come back. Watch in awe as the 200 from Cardiff disintegrate in the face of the Millwall Lions. Aah ... heaven ... I can see it now.

Legalise hooliganism, that's what I say. Why not? I was reading recently that they are thinking of legalising heroin. It is already de-criminalised in some countries. Now what is more destructive? Heroin or hooliganism? A jag from heroin or a jab from a hooligan? I ask you.

League tables would tell us how each firm is getting on each week. Relegation and promotion from the top fight/flight. This would work.

And there are other benefits. Less money for the Old Bill equals less police, so they would have to go and get real jobs and make a positive contribution to society. Plus no one would be fighting anywhere else. They would be saving themselves for the hooligan matches of a weekend. There would be less trouble in bars and clubs up and down the country. Riots would be eliminated from match days in one fell swoop. The country would be a safer place. Police horses could trot around blissfully in gay meadows eternally safe from fireworks. Innocent bystanders could stand by innocently once again. Overturned police cars would be a distant memory. Split visors a thing of the past. The few police at the match would direct the away fans to the Hooli-drome with a pleasant mixture of politeness, envy, relief and a knowledge of the hooli-leagues.

'OK, Cardiff Soul Crew, straight up there and take a left at the top.'

'That is the 'Drome up there, Mr English Bobby, inner?'

'Sure is, by the way, you look like you could be relegated this season, beaten away at Brighton – again.'

'I know inner ... don't fancy our chances much at Millwall today either, inner ...'

So, legalise football hooliganism into organised leagues and much the same as all back-street heroin houses would die off overnight if heroin was legalised; well, all the running battles, street rioting and fighting on match day would be eliminated. Everyone would only want to fight at the big one every week. The organised one.

At the end of the season, the top four go into a round-robin league. The top two go into a big fight-off final. We could hire a fucking big massive arena, say Kenilworth Road. Hmmm. No. Did not go down too well there last time. The Den? No. Unfair advantage to us. Plus there are probably no slots available for The Den to offer out what with all the TV stuff we do these days. Oh yeah – TV. It could get shown on television. We could hold the final at Wembley and the TV audiences would be gigantic.

Two hundred from each firm. No – five hundred for the final. Let us all loose on to the pitch. No knives; no weapons. Everyone is checked before they go on. You have to wear your kit and trainers. The stadium would sell out in a day! Premier Hooli-League Champions – Miiilllwall!

An orgy of violence. We don't mind watching two people fighting in a ring. Even now we are getting more risqué with all that. Cage fighting is one of the fastest-growing sports in the UK, it could be argued. Cage fighting – fucking vicious sport. Now they throw about eight in a ring and the last man standing wins. How much closer to hooliganism can you get? It's the word now – 'hooliganism'. It just conjures up such negative feelings in people. It is like 'tax man', 'cockroach', 'conspiracy', 'Jedward' or 'timeshare'. And, of course, 'Millwall'. All words that just make people recoil and send a shiver down your spine. So a bit of PR and a bit of marketing would be necessary obviously. It is only society's current perspective; if we all work together at this, it would be easy to change.

Then we could expand it into Europe – the Champions League of Hooligans. We could use squad rotations. Blood some of the younger firm members in the knockout Cup games against the likes of Luton at home, resting the top boys for the European Champions Hooli-League Final coming up. And after becoming European champs, you'd then go into the fight-off for the World Club Hooligan Championships. It could become an Olympic sport. We could be the gold medal Olympic winners, paraded on police horseback, the same ones that used to be frightened by our firecrackers. What a turnaround. Rather than the managers and the club being ashamed of us as hooligans, they could present us with the national and international trophies. We could feature in the match programmes once a week – 'Hoolie of the Week'. Instead of Millwall hooligans being derided and faceless, we could be applauded and famous. World Hooligan Champions. We are evil – we are World Champions.

Countries around the world would tune in. Imagine the World Cup of Hooligans. Fuck knows how you would pick our squad? We would all have to put our differences aside and just fight for our country. Wales would be out in the group stages as usual. Scotland would probably go out in the fight-off to make the finals the way they always do. The Irish could be the dark horses. One World Cup we would definitely win. Beware Cuba, though – wouldn't like to get them in the semis.

It would be massive. Of course, reality TV would soon be wanting to jump on the bandwagon. *The Hooligan Factor, Britain's got Hooligans, Ready Steady Kick*, and my favourite, *Hooligans in the Jungle*. You could drop off 100 hardcore hooligans from two firms in the jungle or on a little deserted island. Give them nothing. Nothing at all. Drop them on opposite sides of the island. Tell them they have got a couple of days to prepare. When they hear the klaxon, 'Go find the other firm and go for broke.'

This version is obviously more sadistic – it's potentially a fight to the death and only for the hardcore. They could set booby traps and lure the opposition into their zone. They could make spears and darts to throw poisonous little arrows made from blowfish; slingshots and catapults to fire poisonous stones dipped in viper's venom. Oh, the list is endless. All the big city boys, farmer boys and seasiders fighting to the death on a deserted island. The only way out would be to yell to Ant and Dec (who aren't referees, per se, more observers), 'I'm a fucked hooligan – get me out of here.' It is an idea that has already been floated in the corridors of power. Well, if you can come up with rationalisation. Come on now.

The hooligans are constantly filmed by all the hidden cameras. No real change there then. The audience get to vote two members off each firm every day in the build up to the fight.

So ten days on the island doing their stuff but, each day, two are voted off. After the votes have been cast, 300 riot police bounce on to the island and evict the two members of each firm voted out. They smash into their little huts in the middle of the night. All torches and guns, visors and coshes and drag them from their beds. Kick fuck out of them, spray them with CS gas, then put them on a plane home. Each evictee wins a season ticket for the next year – for their troubles and so as not to press charges against the Met for police brutality.

The audience would love it. Viewing figures would be through the roof. Imagine the public in the build-up to the actual fight. It is all anyone would be talking about up and down the country. Because everyone has that dark side to them; everyone loves that blood and guts story. Ask anyone about Jack the Ripper.

'Oh yes, never caught him, you know?'

Fred West? 'Oh yes. How many did he bury in that house and back garden?'

Millwall? 'Yes, that shower of fucking animals. Animals.'

Dr Shipman? 'Oh yes. They reckon he killed over 200, you know.'

The Yorkshire Ripper? 'Oh yes, Peter Sutcliffe. One sick man.'

Everyone loves that stuff. Intrigued, see. A world they would never enter; same with Hooligan TV.

So why not accept that hooliganism – like prostitution and like drugs – is never going to be eliminated. If we could all accept that, we save a fortune on riot police, we protect cars and horses and save millions for 'all the relevant authorities' from meetings that will no longer be necessary. Then we stick it on TV. We start our own Hooli-telly channel. Then in a return to a sort of Roman gladiatorial spectacle, we let all our best hooligans fight it out. Winner takes all. What TV! What drama!

Then we could combine it with each firm's singing abilities. No, forget that for now. But I stand by the fucking big free-for-all. The ground would be full and the TV audience would be more than when Arthur Fowler went nuts after he had done the Christmas club money. Maybe! More reality TV shows. Just what we need, eh? We could have celebrity hooligans. Watch as Frank Skinner and Adrian Chiles (WBA) have a tag team toe to toe with Oasis duo Liam and Noel (Man City). Bit unfair, really, to tag team Liam with Ricky 'The Hitman' Hatton.

'Eas-y … Eas-y … ' No contest. We could have *International It's a Knockout*. Bring Stuart Hall out of retirement laughing his tits off as he opens the gates to the arena shouting, 'Here come the Belgians.'

Be warned! If no one in authority sees any virtue in broadcasting the Hooli-Leagues, *Celebrity Hooligans* or a reality TV show like *Hooligans in the Jungle* – hooliganism will again raise its ugly head in your civilised society soon!

49

WE'RE FOREVER BURSTING BUBBLES

Then came August 25 2009. In all honesty, when we were drawn away at West Ham in the Carling Cup, I was thinking that the flashing hooligan-ometer would have gone off in the corridors of power. The Football League or the FA, surely one of them would insist the game was played behind closed doors, or on the Isle of Man, or Reykjavik, or the fucking moon. Or at least a 12.00pm kick-off on a Sunday with a ring of steel around it, surely! Given the history, surely they were aware this was a battle waiting to happen.

After all, it is well documented – we hate each other. We had not played each other for over four years. It was a big Cup game. We didn't need Nostradamus – the ball came out the bag and already I was singing that Kaiser Chiefs song 'I Predict a Riot'.

It just shows what little grasp the suits have of the clubs, their histories and the football fans that follow them. This was easily avoidable. Then the (over)reaction afterwards from everyone – the Government, Sports Minister Gerry Sutcliffe, the FA, the Premier League, the Football League, the press, the clubs and old Uncle Tom Cobbly and all. 'Oh what a disgrace!' 'The shame!' 'Football tarnished!' 'A return to the bad old days!'

Bear in mind, of course, these same halfwits had the power to prevent this event, instead of reacting once it had kicked off. All they cared about, of course, was Team England's bid to win the 2018 World Cup. Half a brain between them and they would have known that the planning for this started the minute that ball for Millwall came out of the bag after West Ham's. Phones were going off all over south-east London, both Millwall and West Ham mobiles.

Hundreds went to the stadium without tickets. Hundreds were outside the ground after kick-off. They knew they were not going to get in. West Ham gave us 2,300. We took well over 3,000 fans there. Some estimated even more.

What for? Come on, board room blazers! What for? You honestly could not see this coming? It was totally foreseeable. Just as predictable was the reaction.

'Ban those thugs for life.'

'The punishment should fit the crime.'

'We do not want hooliganism to raise its ugly head again.'

'Banning them is a badge of honour for this scum.'

'They won't care about bans and fines.'

'We don't want a minority wrecking football for all.'

Oh, they all screamed their piece. So none of them, not one ('I predict a riot') nobody amongst all the suits ('I predict a riot'), in all the relevant authorities, never thought for a moment … 'I predict a riot'! Me? I sang it for fucking days.

Poor little Gianfranco Zola. 'I have never seen anything like this,' he said. You want to get down The Den more, Franco. Hooliganism has never left. Did those in charge really believe they had conquered the hooligan element? Get wise. How do you totally conquer it? It is impossible!

Millwall and West Ham, to be fair, do just about all they can to prevent it. But … BUT … when 1,000 cocaine-charged, booze-fuelled, angry, antagonised hooligans face 1,000 cocaine-charged, booze-fuelled, angry, antagonised hooligans with 100 years of vicious, brutal history, do you honestly think a 60-year-old steward in a hi-vis jacket and a 19-year-old policeman straight out of the training academy are going to stop them from clashing?

Oh, the riot I predicted occurred. In all honesty, it could have been much worse. West Ham could have shown up at the meet. Or it could have been at The Den. Then everyone in power after their anticipated reactions were hoping Sepp Blatter's television was on the blink. 'Let's hope he didn't see any of the pictures and will still vote for England's World Cup bid.'

So I guess the police sifted through hours and hours of CCTV footage to 'nail the yobs' who 'fought like animals' in the planned battle. Sports minister Gerry Sutcliffe unsurprisingly called it 'a disgrace to the game ... Football is the loser ... All English fans now travelling abroad will be faced with heavy-handed tactics.' We already were. Cliché city and all utterly predictable. Just like the riot itself.

Of course, the sweetest headline of all for us Millwall boys: 'WE'LL SHUT YOU DOWN – FA THREAT TO CLOSE UPTON PARK AFTER NIGHT OF SHAME'. Mission accomplished. The authorities, of course, always launch a 'full-scale investigation' don't they? All the time, the effort and money poured into that particular investigation could have been avoided so easily. The trouble inside and outside, before, during and after, could have been avoided. I dare say the powers that be had the authority to shut the ground, fine them and sling them out of the competition.

One FA spokesman said, 'We absolutely condemn all the disorder that has occurred at Upton Park. We will be working with all parties, the police and clubs to establish the facts surrounding these events. Every sanction is available.' No shit.

West Ham said they would ban those involved. The chief executive Scott Duxbury said, 'We will leave no stone unturned in identifying the perpetrators, rooting them out and then taking the proper action from both the police point of view and the clubs.' Good luck in finding them, Scott! We have been looking for them for 20 years. The ICF came back for one last hoo-hah. Or is this the start of something big again?

Needless to say, the biggest headlines all carried a similar message: 'WE WON'T LET THE HOOLIGANS RUIN OUR WORLD CUP BID.' The corporate interest rules the game these days. A bid spokesman said, 'England 2018 shares the FA's stance in condemning the disorder surrounding Tuesday's fixture.' Everyone has got to throw their tuppenceworth in. 'The scenes were regrettable but an isolated example of a culture that the football community has worked tirelessly to eradicate from our game. It is extremely disappointing that the mindless actions of a tiny minority have deflected from the passion and dedication that millions of genuine fans show every week for our national game.'

I just have to take umbrage a bit here – it was not mindless action. We had been planning this for ages, as had West Ham's firm. Tiny minority? We had 2,300 tickets and another 1,000 or so outside. The vast majority were ready for a tear-up.

FA Director of Communications Adrian Bevington started banging on about how great they have been, saying, 'We are seen as the leaders ... in the way we have tackled hooliganism over the past 30 years. We receive communications from South America, FIFA, UEFA and other countries asking for advice.'

And what do your communiqués say in reply, Adrian? 'All you have to do to eradicate the problem of hooliganism in your respective countries is bring in all-seater stadia, family zones, community work, better segregation, early kick-offs, road blocks, close all pubs and shops on match day, more stewards, banning orders, all-ticket games, exorbitant prices to turn it into a middle-class game, pass legislation to eliminate all civil liberties, massive fines to all clubs if one fan stumbles over the hoardings on to the pitch, insert CCTV cameras at all locations and, of course, 1,200 riot police at every game with batons, CS gas, plastic bullets, horses, helicopters, dogs, riot vans and impunity. And you will have it cracked. Simples. Bye.' Something like that, is it?

'I am not going to condemn West Ham or Millwall, certainly not at this stage, because we don't know exactly what has been put in place.' And just for the record, why didn't you know what measures had been put in place for this game? Shouldn't you know them off by heart now anyway?

'And we know there have been huge efforts on the part of all our clubs to try to eradicate the problems and we've had a history of success on that. We have to make sure that the individuals concerned face such tough actions that they can't go to football again.'

Andy Williamson, Chief Operating Officer of the Football League, who administer the Carling Cup, was equally bland and predictable. 'We utterly deplore the violence that took place ...' Never, Andy! 'Such behaviour has no place in the game and we will work with all the relevant authorities to ensure that those behind it are held to account.'

We can only guess what work all these relevant authorities accomplished after all the meetings they must have had before the game. I was looking forward to seeing the fruits of their labour after the game.

The only sensible voice I heard came from Football Supporters' Federation Chief Malcolm Clarke. He argued against overreaction. 'It is not a good start to the season and it is important a full investigation is held. But I think we must keep it in perspective ... over the last 20 years, the amount of football violence has radically reduced.' Perspective. Wise words. Hats off, Malcolm.

Sports Minister Gerry Sutcliffe naturally confirmed he would take whatever measures possible to ensure the scenes were not repeated. 'We have made great progress in tackling hooliganism in this country and will not tolerate a return to the dark days of the Eighties.' Could always bring in ID cards and rationalisation, Gerry, rehashing the old Tory policies from the Eighties.

'I completely back the FA's call for any person involved to be banned for life. The scenes last night were a disgrace.' Just to reiterate here – bans mean nothing to any hooligan. They will still be milling around the pubs on their team's derby day, if not for all the games.

Justice Secretary Jack Straw chipped in, saying, 'We have greatly toughened the way police and stewards work. I am determined to ensure what happened here was an aberration.'

Don't make me laugh! OK, Jack, what do you have in mind exactly? Ban the clubs? The fans? Or the game itself? You had 1,200 riot police and you could not control it. What else can you do? Honestly, if one firm wants to kick off against another firm, there is nothing – repeat, nothing – anyone can do. Combine all the authorities, FA, clubs, police, Government, Football League, stewards and every traffic warden in London. When Millwall 'travel' to West Ham, 'if' both firms want to arrange a meet and seriously want to front each other, they will.

So what did the police, football authorities and the clubs do to prevent the firms clashing for the first game against each other in over four years? We know what did not happen – behind closed doors, early kick off, neutral ground, ban away fans. They put 1,200 riot police on duty, combined with three times the normal amount of mounted police. Obviously learnt nothing from the fireworks at Birmingham in 2002. Their chief wig, Met Police Superintendent Steve Wisbey said, 'Police worked closely with West Ham Football Club, British Transport Police and the local authorities to minimise disorder.' A raging success on that front, Steve – congratulations. 'Officers responded swiftly whilst missiles were being thrown as they tried to separate fans outside the ground after the match. Incidents of this nature at a match are thankfully rare but it would appear that a small number of supporters were intent on causing a confrontation.' Stunning eh! Here is the Chief Super virtually admitting they were taken by surprise. 'Officers responded swiftly ...' I can taste and feel his shock that 'a small number of supporters were intent on causing a confrontation'.

So, during this 'working closely with West Ham', were the words 'powder' and 'keg' not used in the same sentence? What was this 'working closely' shit anyway? They phoned or sent a policeman round. 'Pop into West Ham FC and phone the council. They are playing Millwall soon. Oh, remind the council fella our bins at the police station need emptying twice, not once a week. Can you bring me a curry special and a six-pack on your way back?'

West Ham were well aware of the potential for trouble. They even boarded up the Bobby Moore statue, covered it in tarpaulin and paid for a police guard around it, for fuck's sake. They knew what was going to happen.

Of course, the official club statements in the aftermath were as predictable as the riot itself. Theirs said: 'West Ham United continues to investigate the appalling events. Senior club officials are meeting to ensure the appropriate action is taken as swiftly as possible. Video footage, photographic evidence and witness statements are being collated to identify those responsible, while there is ongoing close liaison with all relevant parties including the Met Police and the FA. We will also assist the authorities in their investigation of the mindless violence that took place in the area surrounding the stadium.' Nice to learn of course that it is 'senior club officials' and not just the tea lady and a ticket teller, having a tête-à-tête. Nice, too, West Ham have professional investigators in-house, checking and collating 'video footage, photographic evidence and witness statements ... to identify those responsible'. Nicest of all is the ubiquitous 'close liaison with all the relevant parties'.

Naturally they insisted that every measure was taken to prevent trouble and even 'stressed' there was no fighting in the ground. Fucking great! Even after every measure was taken, still the riot ensued. So it *is* out of their control, then. Oh, and result, too. No fighting inside the ground – well, thousands were running riot outside and fighting battles for hours before, during and after the game. One poor geezer was stabbed. But that's OK, because there was no fighting inside the ground. Three pitch invasions and stewards and police had totally lost control. But it is OK, because there was no fighting inside the ground ... result.

The opening sentence from our club statement was equally as lame: 'Any Millwall supporter identified as being involved in criminal activity relating to the events will receive an indefinite ban from the club ... At the same time, we would like to thank the vast majority of the 2,300 Lions fans at the ground for supporting the team in the appropriate manner.' Then we added smartly: 'We also trust all aspects of planning and preparation for this match will be thoroughly investigated.' Very fucking clever bit of pre-investigation buck-passing by us, methinks.

Really, though, unlucky for West Ham that their ball came

out first. Because if our ball had come out first followed by theirs ... ouch, ouch, ouch!

Police then scrawl through the Internet footage. Of course, all the 'idiot thugs' that turned east London into a 'war zone' will face life bans. The idiotic ones posted videos on YouTube. Then next home game, Old Bill sits there in the CCTV centre scanning every face in the crowd. Anyone they recognise? 20 riot police pile in and take them out, catching him completely by surprise. That is their method these days.

They think by examining all these videos, they can 'identify the ring-leaders'. Of course they can – from West Ham. Although we had members of the firm who had not been out for years that night, unlike every other firm ... We – Do – Not – Have – Ring – Leaders!

So let us just speculate for a moment. Do the police, clubs, FA and all the 'relevant authorities' honestly think if they got lucky and identified 20, 30 or 40 of Millwall's top boys – slapped them all with a life ban – that is it? Problem solved? Honestly, they probably do!

Hypothetical question: Every ... *every* member of *every* firm that goes to make up one big firm – Millwall – *every* member has a life ban; then we draw West Ham at home, sixth round of the FA Cup. Picture 2,000 hardcore hooligans all sat at home on the day of the match twiddling their thumbs, texting and phoning each other.

'Real pity them life bans ... we could have had some fun today.'

'Yes I know, I'm just making some fairy cakes and watching on Sky.'

Get fucking real. With or without a ticket in their pockets, whether they're allowed into the ground or barred, every single one – EVERY SINGLE ONE – would be milling round The Den drinking and preparing themselves for a major kick-off with West Ham. It has been the case since the early part of the last century and it will continue to be the case in the early part of the next century.

Football exists on rivalry; without it, there is no football. That is why so much emphasis is placed on all the derbies that are played throughout the country, Europe and the world. Take that rivalry away. Go on. Take it away. What is left? A sport with no derbies and no grudge matches. Neutrality. All opposition means the same – nothing. No big games, only games. We may as well support no one and oppose no one. A neutral sport. Who wants that?

'Well, I just went to Watford, Birmingham and Sunderland so I'll drive down to Southampton and see how they play tomorrow.' Behave! Without rivalry it is nothing. Locally, nationally, or internationally. No rivalry and it is just a neutral game.

Think Celtic v Rangers; Everton v Liverpool; Real v Barcelona; Inter v AC Milan; England v Germany; England v Scotland. Right. Multiply all these by 1,000, and then do it again. You *still* have not got to the level of rivalry that Millwall v West Ham has. Get the picture? Could always rationalise and amalgamate. Yes, nice one, Maggie.

Another way to solve this problem? Dissolve both clubs – liquidate them, ban them and put us both out of business. Problem solved. Hmm … Millwall v West Ham at rugby, tennis, darts or fucking tiddlywinks and away we go again. It is quite simple. We hate West Ham; West Ham hate us.

Life bans and banning orders are obviously supposed to prevent hooligans from entering the grounds. They do sweet FA! Take it from someone who has served a three-year banning order. We cut our hair, sit in different seats, pull our caps that little bit lower, scarves that little bit higher and we can use someone else's ticket. These are members of the most violent, vicious, evil, hardcore hooligan firm out there. People that are prepared to do some serious shit. Do the authorities really think they are not prepared to breach a banning order?

The answer is no. The FA even admit, 'But if they are found, they can be arrested.' Well there you go. *If* found, *then* arrested. Big fucking deterrent, eh? Given that we are going for a fight, that would also result in 'if found ... you can be arrested'. I wonder how many actually breached the banning order for that night. A fair few is my guess. Some were even posting messages online that they breached existing ones to go to this game. Banning orders can prevent you from travelling abroad. Our firm would have missed out on one game in our history. Crack on with your banning orders.

As the West Ham statement proved, all the clubs want these days is no fighting inside the ground. Half-a-mile away is great for them; it's not their responsibility then. So these banning orders are not designed to prevent hooliganism. Any one that tells you otherwise is a fool or a liar. They are only designed to try and punish one hooligan by trying to prevent him from entering the ground. They are not designed to stop him from meeting the away fans at the station and coshing one over the head. Clubs know this. Everyone knows inside the ground is virtually trouble-free. Hooligans meet elsewhere now – stations or parks or pubs or wherever. Clubs know this. They do not really care about that. They are exonerated of virtually all responsibility because they have done their bit – banned you from the ground.

The Government have to be seen to be tackling it and supporting it. Why? Because even after all these years, they know hooliganism is virtually an unsolvable problem. Even after CCTV, all-ticket games, body searches, early kick-offs, all-seater stadia, police escorts, banning orders, no alcohol on sale, more stewards, away supporters sectioned off, not to mention over 1,000 riot police … when two big firms want to meet, they will. There is no more likelihood of completely stopping or stamping out hooliganism than there is of completely stopping or stamping out crime itself! And every one of the relevant authorities fully understands this. They will never publicly admit it, though. Yet, still, they have to be seen to be tackling and addressing, organising and meeting, resolving and reassuring, blah-blah-blahing and blagging.

West Ham v Millwall in 2009 was made by the press to sound like World War III. The headlines the next day were as sensational as you would expect: 'KICK THEM OUT'; 'FOOTBALL BOSSES WERE URGED TO KICK WEST HAM OUT OF THE COMPETITION'; '1,100 RIOT POLICE TOTALLY LOST CONTROL AS BOTH FIRMS WENT ON THE RAMPAGE'; 'ONE 44-YEAR-OLD GOT STABBED'; 'DOZENS WERE COVERED IN BLOOD AND THIRTEEN ARRESTED ON NIGHT OF SHAME'.

Worse than all the headlines is every bandwagon-jumping politician shouting from the nearest microphone to lambast football's hooligans – cheeky bastards. In the last few decades, you've taken us into The Falklands, Iraq (twice) and Afghanistan. The latter apparently is going to last 40 years. We just want a punch-up. There were no weapons of mass destruction. We just want a punch-up. Am I the only one here that can see the hypocrisy? Punch-up between two firms who want to have a go, versus war. Fucking cheek of the Government.

So what actually happened on Tuesday, 25 August 2009? Well, hardcore fans' websites had arranged that 'meet' in London's Old Street area. 'Bring your bats – and don't bring your kids.' Of course it was pre-planned. This fact appeared to shock most of the relevant authorities. The two firms had planned this! Wow! Text messages, Facebook and websites was how it was done. Plus a few direct phone calls and the good old grapevine. Still going strong despite technological alternatives.

A lot of our older firm members, probably West Ham, too, made a comeback for this game. After all, we had not played each other for over four years. The only correct thing Old Bill did was rate it at a category five – the most serious risk of violence – as soon as we came out of the hat. That is where their good work ended.

West Ham never turned up for the meet. We all jumped the Tube and arrived at Upton Park station at 6.00pm. Hundreds didn't have tickets; hundreds didn't care; hundreds came purely for the fight. So, there is your banning order. Plus loads were probably already banned. West Ham's firm was waiting ... waiting behind police lines.

All sorts of quotes appeared in the papers after that, saying it was really nasty. They had seen nothing like this since the 'bad old' days of the Eighties. Hundreds of 'Wall were walking along with bottles in their hands, looking for their firm, picking a few off here and there. They didn't want to know. Love for Millwall and hatred for West Ham are not in a tap that you can just turn on and off. Everyone was expecting it to go off big time. It never did. West Ham did not want to know us.

The main facts surrounding that day are these: the meet was arranged for Blackhorse Road, 250 Millwall; no-show from West Ham, they did not turn up for the meet; so we went to Barking looking for them; 300 Millwall at Wood Grange Park, some in contact with West Ham an hour before telling them where we would be; again, a no-show from West Ham; Rose Inn Hotel, large numbers of West Ham; over 100 got done; West Ham hid behind the Old Bill outside the ground; West Ham threatened scarfers outside the ground; West Ham stabbed a man who was with his kids; West Ham stood behind Old Bill throwing things – Danny Dyer-wannabe cunts; there were a few kick-offs and a few scuffles; 300 Millwall ran 100 West Ham outside the away turnstile; Millwall broke police lines but West Ham did not want to know; West Ham were 'held back' in the corner by half-a-dozen stewards; Millwall was surrounded by three-deep Old Bill in riot gear; the West Ham fans on the pitch were obviously not hooligans, they were wearing replica shirts; 25,000 West Ham, and 3,000 Millwall; the main firms never met each other on the pitch; they mugged themselves; it was the best Millwall firm for years; shame West Ham had a no show.

If West Ham had shown up at the meet it would have eclipsed anything that had ever happened before in relation to nights of hooliganism. It would have been the most infamous night in hooligan history. The West Ham no-show was a massive disappointment and a big surprise. It had all been pre-arranged away from prying eyes. And they bottled it.

Five months after that night in January 2010, the Football Association fined West Ham £115,000 for failing to control their fans at Upton Park. They were found guilty on two of four charges and had to pay a further £5,000 costs.

We were cleared of all charges.

Fifty people were charged with disorder inside and outside. The FA's disciplinary hearing, a three-man panel chaired by a QC, found West Ham failed to ensure their fans refrained from violent, threatening, obscene and provocative behaviour, and entering the field of play. They were found not guilty of racist behaviour and throwing missiles on to the pitch. We faced the same charges, except for entering the field of play, and all were not proven. We had complained about our ticket allocation.

Our chief executive officer, Andy Ambler, said, 'We have

always maintained that we were innocent of the charges. As ever, this club condemns all misbehaviour within football stadia and works tirelessly to eradicate misconduct and to continue to change an unfair and distorted misconception of Millwall Football Club and its fans.'

Result. Four months later we won promotion through the play-offs, finally. It looked for a while like West Ham could be going down, but just about survived – spared, in more ways than one. So for the 2010/11 season, we could both so nearly have been playing each other in the Championship.

50

HANDLING OLD BILL – A BEGINNER'S GUIDE

Football – I know so many people who don't go anymore. As a kid, I couldn't understand people not going anymore. Now, the way football has degenerated – a once-mighty, working-class, male sport, played and watched by men – has been marketed and priced out of the reach of many of us working-class heroes. Average season ticket prices are now knocking a grand a year. The old man must have his own entrance fee before he takes the two-point-four kids, jumps the train, buys an overpriced pint, cold pie, two Mars bars and two Cokes. It all tots up. One day out for him has got to be well over a ton a game; a couple of grand a season. Less and less people are going to be able to find, let alone justify, that money in the forthcoming years.

No football journalist is going to come out and tell us the bubble is bursting. If they were to start writing that, people would recognise the fact and it would happen even quicker. They gorge on it and live on it, too, remember. But football is dying; it is slowly eating itself through the greed of the clubs, the players and the agents from the inside out. More and more people are saying they have had enough. One day, that will lead to the bubble bursting. Ronaldo going for £80 million! That is not the way football should be.

Sky were great when they first came in – loads more football on television; live games on Fridays, Mondays and Sundays. Now it is total saturation, too many games – two on a Saturday, two or three on a Sunday. Jesus. Stop it, Sky! The saviour of our national sport is going to kill it.

I love eggs. But I don't want to eat seven of a weekend, another few through the week and eight all at once because it is midweek, European egg night. It is just too much; to me, football is just killing itself. And it is fuck-all to do with hooliganism.

I just like to fight. Lots of people go looking for trouble in all walks of life. In the workplace, within the family, when out socialising, on the streets, lots of people do it for a living and we applaud them because the Marquess of Queensbury set down a few rules. People who want to can find trouble in an empty room. It is not dependent on how big your house was on the day you were born, how much money was in the parents' bank account, how high up the social ladder you are, nor any other of a million and one reasons – people fight and realise they like it. Win, lose or draw, they want to do it more. Football firms in the main are working-class kids from tough, inner-city areas. We may all have things that are different from each other, but all have one thing in common – we all like to fight.

As football fans, our basic rights are booted out the back door as soon as we leave our house on match day. The police have unlimited powers and they treat us like shit. If you get arrested, keep calm, and remember these points:

• There is no such thing as a friendly chat, so say fuck-all.

They can stop anyone at any time; forget all that needing 'reasonable suspicion' bullshit.

- Ask to see their warrant card, why you have been stopped and, at the end, ask for a record of the search.
- Don't resist a search because you run the risk of both injury and further charges.
- At the police station, you always have the right to be treated humanely, to speak to the custody officer, to have someone notified of your arrest, to consult with a solicitor and to see the written codes governing rights and how we are treated.
- They can only keep you for a certain period of time, so make sure the correct time for your arrest is on the custody record.
- Make sure you know why you've been arrested because the Old Bill could arrest you and make something up later.
- Insist on seeing a solicitor and ask them to be present at your interview.
- If anything you ask for is refused, ensure it is on the custody record.
- Reply 'no comment' to all questions.
- Don't write or sign any statement until you have seen a solicitor.
- If you are at the football, do not accept a caution under any circumstances as it's an admission of guilt.
- If the Old Bill come to your house, they can use reasonable force to gain entry. You are entitled to see a copy of any search warrant and a record of the search must be kept by police.
- Make sure you are present and when police take your possessions insist on a written list of all items seized.
- If you hear: 'You don't have to say anything but it may harm your defence,' reply with: 'I've been advised not to

answer as it's not right to attempt to defend myself until charges have been made and that I have a solicitor present to ensure all questions are fair and legal.'

- Get a brief, he will advise you when to respond and when not to.
- Challenge everything the police do, make a written record and get it witnessed, dated and signed.
- Take photos of any property damaged and ensure all injuries are medically examined.
- Most of all, keep calm.

Many years ago while on holiday in the Canary Islands, I was stood in a bar chatting with some Dutch guy. The topic turned to football and he was telling me all about his club – Ajax of Amsterdam. He then asked me, 'So who do you support?'

'You won't have heard of my team ... it's only a small club in London. We are Millwall.'

'Ah, Millwall ... the greatest hooligans in the world also.'
I agreed.

51

THE LIONS' ROAR – MILLWALL'S CHANTS

The lions, the lions
Da-da-da-da-da-da-da-da-da-da ... roar (war)

Berty Mee said to Bill Shankly,
'Have you heard of the North Bank Highbury?'
Shanks said, 'I don't think so,
But I've heard of the Millwall aggro.'

I was born under the Cold Blow Lane
Oh, I was born under the Cold Blow Lane
Boots are made for kicking, kicking in the head
I won't stop fucking kicking until the fucking bastard's dead
Knives are made for stabbing, stabbing in the head
I won't stop fucking stabbing until the fucking bastard's dead
Oh, South London's wonderful, Oh, South London's wonderful
It full of tits, fanny and Millwall, Oh, South London's
wonderful.

Bobby Moore, Bobby Moore, riding through the glen
Bobby Moore, Bobby Moore, with his merry men

Queer as a cunt, takes it up the bum
Bobby Moore, he's no more, Bobby Moore.

Bobby Moore, Bobby Moore, running from The Den
Bobby Moore, Bobby Moore, he has sex with men
Queer as they come, takes it up the bum
Bobby Moore, he's no more, Bobby Moore.

If I had the wings of a sparrow
If I had the arse of a crow
I'd fly over West Ham tomorrow
And then shit on the bastards below, below,
And shit on the bastards below.

Chim chimney, chim chimney, chim chim cherroo
We hate those bastards in claret and blue.

When I was just a little boy
I asked my father what will I be,
Will I be Arsenal? Will I be Spurs?
Here's what he said to me:
Millwall ... Millwall ... Millwall ... Millwall.

Hello, hello, we are the Millwall boys
Hello, hello, we are the Millwall boys
If you are a West Ham fan
Surrender or you'll die
'Cos we all follow the Millwall.

'Ello, 'ello ... Millwall aggro
'Ello, 'ello ... Millwall aggro

My old man said be a West Ham fan
I said, 'Fuck off, bollocks, you're a cunt,'
We'll take East London and all that's in it
We'll take The Boleyn with the West Ham in it
With axes and hammers, carving knives and spanners
We'll show those bastards how to fight.
'Cos you'll never take The Den with The Bushwackers in it
'Cos we're the pride of South London.

Harry Roberts is our friend
Is our friend, is our friend,
Harry Roberts is our friend
He kills coppers.
Let 'im out he'll kill some more
Kill some more, kill some more,
Harry Roberts.

Fuck 'em all, fuck 'em all
United, West Ham, Liverpool
'Cos we are the Millwall and we are the best
We are the Millwall so fuck all the rest
Fuck 'em all.

A final thought – a bit of perspective:

In AD 532, rivalry between supporters of the blue and green chariot-racing teams in Constantinople led to 30,000 deaths in the week of the Nika riots.